Edexcel GCSE

History A: The Making of the Modern World

Unit 2A Germany 1918–39

Student Book

John Child
Series editors: Nigel Kelly • Angela Leonard

Contents: delivering the Edexcel GCSE History A (The Making of the Modern World) specification Unit 2A

edexcel

Welcome to the course

Welcome to Modern World History! Studying this subject will help you to understand the world you live in: the events of the last century can help to explain the problems and opportunities that exist in the world today.

There are four units in the course and each is worth 25% of the whole GCSE. Those units are:

- Unit 1 Peace and War: International Relations 1900–91
- Unit 2 Modern World Depth Study (Germany 1918–39; Russia 1917–39; or USA 1919–41)
- Unit 3 Modern World Source Enquiry (First World War and British Society 1903–28; Second World War and British Society 1931–51; or the USA 1945–70)
- Unit 4 Representations of History (your controlled assessment task).

Introduction to Unit 2A

This book covers Unit 2A: Germany 1918–39. This is the 'Depth Study' section of your course, in which you study just one country, Germany. Focusing on this country means you will be able to understand in more detail the uneasy birth of the Weimar Republic and its rocky path through the 1920s, Hitler's astounding rise to power, the Nazi police state and what Nazi Germany was like.

The exam for this section lasts 1 hour 15 minutes and you must answer three questions. The questions test your knowledge of what happened, through your understanding of the causes and consequences of events, and the key features of what happened.

In the Unit 2 exam, you will also be assessed on your spelling, punctuation and grammar (Questions 2 and 3) and on the quality of your written communication (Question 3).

How to use this book

There are four key topics in this book and you have to study all of them for the exam.

- Key Topic 1: The Weimar Republic 1918–33
- Key Topic 2: Hitler and the growth of the Nazi Party 1918–33
- Key Topic 3: The Nazi dictatorship 1933–39
- Key Topic 4: Nazi domestic policies 1933–39

These key topics are the heart of this book (pages 6–73). When you understand them, there is a further section in the book, examzone, to help you prepare for the exam.

Key terms are emboldened in the text, and definitions can be found in the glossary.

We've broken down the six stages of revision to ensure you are prepared every step of the way.

Zone in: how to get into the perfect 'zone' for revision.

Planning zone: tips and advice on how to plan revision effectively.

Know zone: the facts you need to know, memory tips and exam-style practice for every section.

Don't panic zone: last-minute revision tips.

Exam zone: what to expect on the exam paper.

Zone out: what happens after the exams.

Results**Plus**

These features help you to understand how to improve, with guidance on answering exam-style questions, tips on how to remember important concepts and how to avoid common pitfalls.

There are three different types of ResultsPlus features throughout this book:

Top Tips provide handy hints on how to apply what you have learned and how to remember key information and concepts.

Results Plus
Top Tip

The above question is about *key features*. Students who do well in these questions organise their information.
You need to make sure you identify a key feature and then provide information about it. For example, what information would you give about:
● the failure of the Putsch on the day
● the longer-term results?
There was a key features question on page 21. Use the advice there to help you here.

Watch out! These warn you about common mistakes and misconceptions that students often make.

Results Plus
Watch out!

Some students confuse the *chancellor* and the *president*.
The *chancellor* was:
● the head of the German *government* – rather like our prime minister.
The *president* was:
● the head of the German *state* – rather like our queen or king.

Build Better Answers give you an opportunity to answer exam-style questions. They include tips for what a basic ■, good ● and excellent △ answer will contain.

Results Plus
Build Better Answers

Exam question: Describe how the Weimar Republic was governed.

(6 marks)

Your exam paper will always have a question like this one, which tests your ability to *select* and *communicate* factual information.

■ **A basic answer (level 1)** gives points without detail (for example, *The government was democratic*).

● **A good answer (level 2)** gives details to support each point (for example, *The government was more democratic than under the Kaiser, because men and women over 20 years could vote*).

△ **An excellent answer (full marks)** gives three points, each with supporting detail.

The Know Zone Build Better Answers pages at the end of each section include an exam-style question with a student answer, examiner comments and an improved answer so that you can see how to improve your own writing.

Results Plus
Build Better Answers

Question 1 (a)
Tip: Question 1 (a) will ask you to make an inference from a source and provide evidence from the source to support it.
Let's look at an example. On page 13 you are told:
In September 1923 a new chancellor was appointed – Gustav Stresemann. In November 1923 he cancelled the old mark and issued a new currency – the Rentenmark. This led to a period of stability.
A suitable question for this source would be:

What does this source tell us about Germany in 1923? (4 marks)

Student answer	Examiner comments
This source tells me that Stresemann was appointed in 1923 and that he introduced a new currency, the Rentenmark. It also tells me that he took over a country that had many problems.	The first part of this answer merely repeats information contained in the source, so it would be marked in the bottom level. The last sentence does make an inference (a judgment which is not actually stated in the source) when it says that the country had many problems. But it does not say what in the source makes it possible to make that inference.

Let's rewrite the answer with that additional detail.

| This source tells me that Stresemann was appointed in 1923 and that he introduced a new currency, the Rentenmark. It also tells me that he took over a country that had many problems. I know this because he had to cancel the old currency and introduce a new one. You don't do serious things like that unless there is a real problem. It also says it led to stability – so that proves that before there must have been instability. | An inference is made and two pieces of support are given; this is enough for 4 marks. |

Key Topic I:
The Weimar Republic, 1918–33

By 1918, the Germans had been at war – the First World War – for four years. They had faced the combined might of the Allies – Britain, France, Russia, Italy and the USA. The Allied navies were blockading Germany, preventing imports. There were shortages of weapons for troops and basic supplies for the population. The Germans launched a last desperate attack upon Paris in the spring of 1918 – but failed.

Food shortages caused severe hardship and military failures caused a sense of hopelessness. All this created public unrest all over Germany. Workers at the Daimler plant, in Stuttgart, went on strike and demonstrated in the streets. In Munich, there was an uprising led by a Jewish communist, named Kurt Eisner. In several cities workers set up their own local government councils. In Hanover, soldiers refused to control rioters and, in Kiel and Hamburg, naval crews refused to follow orders and mutinied.

Therefore, by November 1918, many parts of Germany were in revolt and it was clear that the war was lost. The Army told the German Emperor (the Kaiser) that he had to abdicate – firstly to save the country from civil war and secondly because the Allies would be less harsh on a new, more democratic government. So, on 9 November 1918, Kaiser Wilhelm accepted his fate and fled to Holland. Germany's biggest political party, the Social Democrat Party (SPD) took power. Since it was first unified in 1871, Germany had been an autocracy – ruled by one person – the Kaiser. But the SPD now declared Germany a democratic republic, soon known as the Weimar Republic. Friedrich Ebert, an SPD leader, became its first chancellor.

In this Key Topic you will study:

- the origins and early problems of the Weimar Republic, 1918–23
- the recovery of the Weimar Republic under Stresemann, 1924–29
- the impact of the Great Depression, 1929–33.

The Weimar Republic faced many problems in its early years. There were economic problems caused by the effects of the war; there were revolts against the new government. From 1924 the work of Chancellor Stresemann seemed to bring prosperity back to Germany. But this came to a dramatic end after 1929 when economic depression destroyed both the German economy and the Weimar Republic.

The Treaty of Versailles

Learning objectives

In this chapter you will learn about:

● the Treaty of Versailles – its terms and effects

● reasons for German resentment of the treaty.

The Diktat

On 11 November 1918, just two days after the Kaiser had abdicated, Matthias Erzberger, representing the new government, signed the armistice – an agreement to stop fighting. The Allied leaders – David Lloyd George (Britain), Georges Clemenceau (France) and Woodrow Wilson (United States) – then drew up the peace treaty.

The Germans were given 15 days to respond to the treaty. It said Germany had to accept the blame for starting the war, pay **reparations** (compensation) to the victorious nations and agree to reductions in Germany's armed forces and territory.

THE STAR, WEDNESDAY, FEBRUARY 2, 1921.

Some Steeplechase.

Source B: *a cartoon from* The Star *in 1921. When reparations were fixed, in 1921, even the British press could see that they were too high.*

The Germans were bitterly opposed and asked for several changes; all were refused. The treaty was a **diktat** – they were not invited to the negotiations and the treaty was imposed upon them. Because of their military collapse, and economic and political turmoil, they had to accept. On 28 June 1919, the German delegation signed the Treaty of Versailles.

The treaty was not liked by the German people or German political parties. They blamed Germany's new political leaders for signing the treaty. This link with defeat and humiliation weakened the new republic right from the very start.

The victors demand that we, as the defeated, shall be made to pay, and, as the guilty, we shall be punished. The demand is that we should agree that we, alone, are guilty of having caused the war. Such a confession, in my mouth, would be a lie.

Source A: *Count Brockdorff-Rantsau, leader of the German delegation at Versailles.*

Vengeance, German nation! Today, in the Hall of Mirrors at Versailles, a disgraceful treaty is being signed. Never forget it! On that spot…German honour is being dragged to its grave. There will be revenge for the shame of 1919.

Source C: *from* Deutsche Zeitung, *a German newspaper, 28 June 1919.*

Activities

1 Put yourself in the place of Chancellor Ebert. Use the information on these two pages and write a reply to the *Deutsche Zeitung* explaining why you had to sign the Treaty of Versailles.

The terms of the Treaty of Versailles

Germany had to pay reparations to the Allies

- Reparations were eventually fixed, in 1921, at 136,000 million marks (£6600 million)

Germany lost all its colonies

- The 11 German colonies in Africa and the Far East were given to victorious countries as 'mandates' – territories to look after

German military forces were cut

- The army was limited to 100,000; to be used internally only
- The navy was limited to 6 battleships, 6 cruisers, 12 destroyers and 12 torpedo boats. No submarines were allowed. The rest of the fleet was destroyed
- No air force was allowed. The existing air force was destroyed
- The Rhineland was demilitarised
  - the German army was not allowed in the Rhineland, which bordered France

Germany lost land

- Alsace and Lorraine were lost to France
- Eupen and Malmédy were lost to Belgium
- Posen and West Prussia were lost to Poland
  - the loss of Posen and West Prussia divided Germany in two, cutting off East Prussia from the rest of the country
- Plebiscites (public votes) had to take place in other areas, to decide whether they should leave Germany
  - Upper Silesia voted to become part of Poland
  - Northern Schleswig decided to become part of Denmark
- The German port of Danzig was made an international city – not governed by Germany
- The output of the rich Saar coalfields was also to go to France for 15 years
- Altogether, Germany lost:
  - about 13% of its European territory
  - almost 50% of its iron and 15% of its coal reserves

Germany and the Treaty of Versailles

Dolchstoss – the stab in the back

The Treaty of Versailles was particularly unpopular because the German people believed that their army had never been defeated in the war. It had failed to win but it had not been defeated. Critics of the treaty claimed that the army had been ready to fight on. They said that the army had been betrayed by politicians in Berlin – in effect, that they had been 'stabbed in the back' (the Dolchstoss).

Even Ebert, the new chancellor, greeted the return of the German Army to Berlin in December 1918 with the words *'Your sacrifice and deeds are without parallel. No enemy defeated you!'* Ebert had to accept the peace but he had lost two sons who were soldiers in the war and he never accepted defeat.

The politicians who signed the Treaty were blamed for its harsh terms. These politicians became known as the '**November Criminals**' and resentment followed the new republic all the way to its collapse in 1933.

The treaty therefore had lasting effects within Germany.

- It weakened the popularity of the Weimar Republic.
- It caused lasting political protest (see pages 14–17).
- It harmed Germany's economy (see pages 12–13).

Source D: *a poster from 1931 showing a German with his hands chained by the shackles of Versailles. Even 12 years after the treaty was signed, parties campaigned against it.*

ResultsPlus

Build Better Answers

Exam question: Explain why the Germans disliked the Treaty of Versailles. (8 marks)

The examination will always have questions on *why things happened* – like this one.

■ **A basic answer (level 1)** gives one or two reasons why the Germans disliked the treaty, but without detail (for example, *One reason why the Germans hated the treaty was that they had to pay reparations. Another reason was because Germany lost land*).

● **A good answer (level 2)** gives detailed information to illustrate each reason (for example, *One reason why the Germans hated the treaty was that they had to pay reparations adding up to £6600 million. Another reason was because Germany lost land. In all, Germany lost about 13% of its European territory*).

▲ **A better answer (level 3)** explains why each reason was unpopular (for example, *Losing Posen divided Germany into two parts, cutting off East Prussia completely*).

▲ **An excellent answer (full marks)** shows links between reasons (for example, *The Germans didn't like being blamed for the war. They thought this was unfair. But also this blame meant they had to pay reparations, which they also disliked*). The answer then gives details of reparations and why they were disliked).

The Weimar Republic – a new constitution

Learning objectives

In this chapter you will learn about:

● how a new constitution was agreed

● the terms of the new Weimar constitution

● the weaknesses of the constitution.

After the Kaiser's departure, there was unrest all around Germany. Armed groups with extreme political views clashed with the army and even claimed control in some towns. But Ebert began to take control by introducing slow, careful changes. Civil servants stayed in post. Six moderate social democrats formed a Council of People's Representatives, a temporary government. They organised elections for a National Assembly. This met in February 1919 to create a new **constitution**. With so much unrest in Berlin, the Assembly met in Weimar – and the new republic was called the Weimar Republic, even after the government moved back to Berlin. By August 1919 the Assembly had drawn up the new constitution.

The terms of the constitution

The constitution was more **democratic** than government under the Kaiser. German people had more control.

There was also a system of **checks and balances**. This meant that power was shared out (see below).

Local government was run by the 18 regions of Germany (e.g. Bavaria, Prussia); they kept local parliaments.

Central government was given more power than before.

The **Reichstag** was the dominant house of the new German parliament; it controlled taxation.

● Members of the Reichstag were elected every four years.

● All men and women over 20 years could vote, using a secret ballot.

● **Proportional representation** was used. This meant that the number of Reichstag seats which political parties were given depended on the percentage of votes they gained.

The **Reichsrat**: the other house of the German parliament.

● A number of members were sent by each local region, according to its size.

● The Reichsrat could delay new laws unless overruled by a two-thirds majority of the Reichstag.

The **chancellor** was the head of the government.

● The chancellor chose ministers and ran the country.

● But to pass laws, he needed majority support in the Reichstag.

The **president** was the head of state; the president was directly elected by the people every seven years.

● The president took no part in day-to-day government.

● But the president was a powerful figure.

  – He chose the chancellor (usually the leader of the largest party).

  – He could dismiss the Reichstag, call new elections and assume control of the army.

  – Also, under Article 48, the president could suspend the constitution, and pass laws by decree.

Source A: *armed protesters parading in Berlin in 1919.*

Friedrich Ebert was elected by the Assembly as the first president. He carefully gained the support of powerful groups in society.

- He promised General Gröner, the head of the German Army, that there would be no reform of the armed forces.
- He reassured the industrialists' leader, Hugo Stinnes, that there would be no nationalisation of private businesses.
- He ensured the support of trade unions by promising their leader, Karl Legien, a maximum eight-hour working day.

With this support, the new government overcame the opposition of the protesters and gradually gained control of the country. The new republic was successfully launched but it had its weaknesses.

Weaknesses of the constitution

Firstly, proportional representation meant that even a party with a small number of votes gained seats in the Reichstag. During the 1920s, 28 parties were represented in the Reichstag. To get majority support, chancellors needed **coalitions** of several parties – usually the Social Democrats, the People's Party, the Democratic Party and the Centre Party.

But these all wanted different things, making stable government difficult.

Secondly, the careful balancing of powers made strong, decisive government by the chancellor very difficult in times of crisis.

This second weakness meant that, whenever compromise broke down, the chancellor had to ask the president to suspend the constitution, under Article 48, and rule by decree. This gave the impression that the new constitution didn't really work.

The Weimar Republic was built on shaky foundations. Extremist parties didn't support it; moderate Germans feared it was too weak.

Source B: *a 1950s painting of Ebert addressing the National Assembly in the National Theatre, Weimar, 1919.*

ResultsPlus
Build Better Answers

Exam question: Describe how the Weimar Republic was governed. **(6 marks)**

Your exam paper will always have a question like this one, which tests your ability to *select* and *communicate* factual information.

■ **A basic answer (level 1)** gives points without detail (for example, *The government was democratic*).

● **A good answer (level 2)** gives details to support each point (for example, *The government was more democratic than under the Kaiser, because men and women over 20 years could vote*).

▲ **An excellent answer (full marks)** gives three points, each with supporting detail.

Did you know?

Because the National Assembly could not meet in Berlin, its meetings were held in Weimar's National Theatre, complete with stage, circle and box seats.

Economic problems, 1918–23

> **Learning objectives**
>
> In this chapter you will learn about:
> - the bankruptcy of the new Weimar government
> - the occupation of the Ruhr
> - inflation and hyperinflation.

Bankruptcy

At first, Germany's biggest problem was that its government was bankrupt; its reserves of gold had all been spent in the war. The Treaty of Versailles made things worse. It deprived Germany of wealth-earning areas, such as coalfields in Silesia. It also made the German government pay reparations. Germany asked for reductions, but the victors, especially France, needed money to pay war debts to the USA. With no gold reserves and falling income, by 1923 Germany could no longer pay.

Occupation of the Ruhr

In retaliation, the French sent troops into the German industrial area of the Ruhr (see the map on page 8). They confiscated raw materials, manufactured goods and industrial machinery. The German government urged passive resistance; workers went on strike; there was even some sabotage. The French replied by arresting those who obstructed them and bringing in their own workers.

The Germans bitterly resented what the French had done. However, many Germans also resented the failure of the Weimar Republic to resist, even though, realistically, they had no choice. Germany's reduced troop numbers of 100,000 were no match for the 750,000 in the French Army.

The occupation of the Ruhr did the French little good, but it crippled Germany. Many factories and around 80 per cent of German coal, iron and steel were based there. The disruption increased Germany's debts, unemployment and the shortage of goods.

Inflation

These shortages meant that the price of things went up – this is called **inflation**. People had to pay more money to get what they needed.

The government needed money to pay their debts, but unemployment and failing factories meant they received less money from taxes. During 1919–23, government income was only a quarter of what was required, so the government just printed more money. In 1923, the government had 300 paper mills and 2000 printing shops just to print more money.

Source A: *this 1923 poster shows German bitterness. France is seen ravaging German industry. The caption reads 'Hands off the Ruhr area!'*

Source B: *German cartoon from 1922 – Gutenberg, the German inventor of the printing press, says 'This I did not want!'*

This made it easier initially for the government to pay reparations but it made inflation even worse. It was a vicious circle: the more prices rose, the more money was printed and this made prices rise again. By 1923, prices reached spectacular heights. A loaf of bread cost 1 mark in 1919; by 1922 it cost 200 marks; by November 1923 it cost 200,000 billion marks. This extreme inflation is called hyperinflation.

The results of hyperinflation were complex.

- **Everyone suffered from shortages**. This was because German marks became worthless in comparison with foreign currency. In 1918, £1 cost 20 marks; by November 1923, £1 cost 20 billion marks. Foreign suppliers refused to accept marks for goods, so imports dried up and shortages of food and other goods got worse – for everyone.

- **Everyone found it difficult to buy what they needed** – even if their wages went up. People had to carry bundles of money in baskets and even wheelbarrows. Many workers were paid twice a day – so they could rush out and buy goods before prices rose even further. Some suppliers refused to take money at all, asking for payment in kind (swapping goods).

- **People with savings** were hit hardest – those with money in bank accounts, insurance policies or pensions; their savings became worthless. Those affected were mainly from the middle classes.

However, there were those who benefited as well: big businessmen and industrialists, who had borrowed heavily, profited as the real value of their debts plummeted; others did well by hoarding goods; foreign visitors profited as the value of their own country's currency rose against the German mark.

Eventually, things improved. In August 1923, a new chancellor was appointed – Gustav Stresemann. In November 1923, he cancelled the old mark and issued a new currency – the Rentenmark. This led to a period of stability (see page 18).

However, most Germans had suffered and many blamed the Weimar Republic. The middle classes had suffered most; they should have been the bedrock of support for the Weimar Republic.

> On days when Mutti was not able to buy bread, she searched through the garbage cans for potato peels and other scrap… [or]…she took kitchen scraps and leftovers from the houses where she did laundry.

Source C: from On Hitler's Mountain, by Irmgard Hunt – her mother lived in 1920s Germany.

Examination question

Explain why there was so much social hardship in Germany between 1918 and 1923. (8 marks)

Tip: This is a *causation* question – about *why* things happened. There will always be a causation question in your examination. There is advice about how to tackle this type of question on page 9.

Activity

- Write the following on small cards: fall in value of pensions; shortage of industrial goods; government bankruptcy; fall in value of savings; inflation; reparations; occupation of the Ruhr; printing more money; loss of land after Versailles.
- Organise the cards into causes and effects. Draw lines to link causes and their effects. (Note: some cards may be both a cause of one thing and an effect of another.)
- What does the resulting diagram tell you about:
  - the causes of the bankruptcy of the German government
  - the causes of the social and economic problems of the German people?

Political problems, 1918-23

Learning objectives

In this chapter you will learn about:

- the main political groups in the Weimar Republic
- the political unrest in the Weimar Republic during 1918–23.

Source A: *this right-wing cartoon shows Karl Liebknecht, leader of Germany's communists, attacking German property, industry, money and families.*

The start of the Weimar Republic was marked by political unrest all over Germany. This unrest came from right-wing and left-wing groups.

Right wing and left wing

Those on the right wing of politics:

- want to keep society very stable
- want a strong government dominated by powerful leaders
- support capitalism – the private ownership of land and business
- stress the importance of the family unit, law and order and traditional values
- are nationalist – placing the interests of the nation over the individual.

Fascism and Nazism are extreme right-wing movements.

Generally, those on the left wing of politics:

- want to change society rapidly
- aim to treat all people as equals and give political power to workers
- oppose capitalism; they want to abolish private ownership of land or business and put these in the hands of workers
- are internationalist; they stress co-operation of nations.

Socialists are left wing. Communism is an extreme left-wing movement.

Did you know?

The terms 'left' and 'right' to describe political views date back to the French Revolution. In the new 1789 parliament, members who wanted to limit change and keep power in the hands of the king and a small elite sat on the king's right. Those who wanted to change the political system and give the people more power sat on the king's left.

At this time, the right wing in German politics included many small nationalist parties.

- They resented that the Weimar Republic's Social Democrat politicians had abandoned the army in 1918.
- Even more, they hated the communists who had undermined the Kaiser with riots and mutinies in 1918.
- They feared the damage communists would do to their property and German traditions.
- They wanted to reverse Versailles, reinstate the Kaiser, boost the army and return Germany to her former strength.
- They gained support from the military, the judiciary and the civil service, who were opposed to giving power to ordinary people in the new, democratic Weimar Republic.

The left wing in Germany was dominated by the KPD, the Communist Party of Germany.

- They wanted a revolution in Germany like the one in Russia in 1917.
- They thought that the Weimar Republic gave too little power to the workers.
- They wanted government by councils of workers or soldiers.
- They wanted to abolish the power in Germany of the land-owning classes and the army.

From 1918–23, the German people were unhappy about:

- the Weimar leaders' decision not to fight on in 1918
- the 1919 Treaty of Versailles, which Germans regarded as punitive and vindictive
- the hardships caused by unemployment and inflation.

All this persuaded many people in Germany to support extreme left-wing or right-wing political groups between 1918 and 1923. If they did support extremist groups, German workers tended to support the socialists and communists, while the German Army, business classes and landowners tended to support the right-wing groups.

Source B: *a left-wing political poster produced by the KPD – Communist Party of Germany. They portray themselves as the slayers of German capitalism, militarism and the German landed nobility – the Junker. The Spartacists were part of the Communist Party.*

The main political parties in the Weimar Republic

KPD	SPD	DDP	ZP	DVP	DNVP	NSDAP
Communist Party	Social Democrats	Democratic Party	Centre Party	People's Party	National Party	Nazi Party
Extreme left wing	Moderate left wing	Left wing Liberal	Moderate	Right wing Liberal	Right wing	Extreme right wing
Opposed Weimar Republic	Supported Weimar Republic	Supported Weimar Republic	Supported Weimar Republic	Supported Weimar Republic in 1920s	Opposed Weimar Republic	Opposed Weimar Republic
Supported by workers and some middle classes	Supported by workers and middle classes	Backed by business	Originally the party of the Catholic Church	Backed by upper middle classes	Landowners, wealthy middle class and big business	See pp28-29 and 36-39.

Violent political unrest

One thing which made politics in the Weimar Republic so violent was that political parties had their own private armies. They recruited mainly ex-soldiers, who were often unemployed and bitter that their government had accepted peace. The left wing had its Rotfrontkämpfer (Red Front Fighters). The Stahlhelm (Steel Helmets – a veterans' group) were a conservative organisation on the right wing. Even the moderate SPD had its Sozi force.

At first, private armies were for protection, but they quickly caused political activity to become violent.

- Hugo Haasse, one of Ebert's Council of People's Representatives, was murdered in 1919.
- Matthias Erzberger, a moderate politician who signed the surrender of Germany in 1918, was shot and killed walking in the Black Forest in August 1921.
- Walther Rathenau, the Weimar foreign minister, was machine-gunned to death in the street in Berlin in June 1922.

In all, between 1919 and 1922 there were 376 political murders, mostly of left-wing or moderate politicians. However, not a single right-wing murderer was convicted and executed; ten left-wing assassins were. This shows how much the judiciary (the legal system) was filled with right-wing supporters.

> The Social Democratic politicians into whose lap the German government fell in 1918 didn't have widespread support. Instead, they faced a bitter, suffering population, filled with unrealistic ideas about what peace could bring and divided about…the road ahead.

Source C: *from* Nazism and War, *Richard Bessel (2004)*

The Spartacist League (a left-wing movement)

Sometimes extreme political groups tried to overthrow the government by force. For example, during the winter of 1918–19 there were left-wing uprisings throughout Germany, which set up workers' and soldiers' soviets – local councils – in towns across Germany. A central Council of Commissars was created, claiming to be the true government, as a direct threat to the new moderate government of Ebert in Berlin.

The most influential communist leaders were Rosa Luxemburg and Karl Liebknecht, organisers of the Spartacist League – named after Spartacus, the head of a slaves' revolt in Ancient Rome. On 6 January 1919, inspired by the Spartacists, 100,000 communists demonstrated in Berlin and took over key buildings, such as newspaper offices.

Chancellor Ebert, and his defence minister, Gustav Noske, needed to put down the rebels. They realised that the regular army (the Reichswehr) was in no shape to put down the revolt alone, so they turned to the **Freikorps.**

The Freikorps were demobilised soldiers, returning from the war, who had refused to give back their arms. They were anti-communist and worked with the regular army. It is estimated that the Freikorps numbered 250,000 by March 1919.

Source D: *a recruitment poster for the Freikorps, 1919.*

With the help of the Freikorps, the Weimar government was able to put down the Spartacist uprisings in early 1919. Several thousand communist supporters were arrested or killed, mostly in Berlin. Both Rosa Luxemburg and Karl Liebknecht were arrested on 15 January and both were murdered by the Freikorps. Leibknecht was shot; Luxemburg was shot in the head and her body dumped in a canal.

The Kapp Putsch (a right-wing revolt)

But the unrest continued. In 1920, 5000 right-wing supporters of Dr Wolfgang Kapp marched on Berlin to overthrow the Weimar Republic and bring back the Kaiser. For a while, the rebels controlled the city. The government fled to Dresden; they urged people not to co-operate and instead go on strike.

Many workers obliged – they had socialist leanings and no desire to see the Kaiser return. Essential services – gas, electricity, water, transport – stopped and the capital ground to a halt. Kapp realised he could not govern and fled. He was caught and put in prison, where he later died.

Still the unrest continued. In 1923, there was another right-wing uprising – the Munich Putsch – led by Adolf Hitler (see pages 30–31).

Unrest subsides

It wasn't until the end of 1923 that the political unrest calmed down. A new chancellor, Gustav Stresemann, came to power; inflation was brought under control; suffering was reduced and politics became more moderate (see pages 18–21).

However, by this time, the Weimar Republic was permanently weakened by the political unrest.

- It had not been able to govern on its own authority. It relied upon workers' strikes and the violence of the Freikorps. Government forces had killed thousands of Germans to keep themselves in power.
- Extremist parties had gathered strength during the turbulent years of 1918–23. They still had their private armies and events had taught the worrying lesson that those with most military power could eventually win.

Examination question

Describe the ways political unrest was dealt with in Germany in the years 1919–20. **(6 marks)**

Tip: This is a question where you *select* information and *communicate* it. There will always be a question like this in your exam. There is advice about this type of question on page 11.

17

ResultsPlus
Watch out!

Exam candidates sometimes get confused between right-wing and left-wing movements. Use the tip below to help you remember.

- The Spartacist **L**eague was a **L**eft-wing organisation.
- The Kapp Putsch (**R**evolt) was a **R**ight-wing uprising.

Source E: *armed Freikorps soldiers, an armoured car and a flame-thrower, putting down unrest in Berlin during 1920.*

Activity

- As a class or a group, draw up a balance sheet of successes and failures for the Weimar Republic by 1923.
- Overall, how had it done?

Weimar recovery, 1924–29: the Stresemann era

> ### Learning objectives
>
> In this chapter you will learn about:
> - Stresemann's reforms to end the currency crisis
> - reducing reparations: the Dawes Plan and Young Plan
> - successes abroad: the League of Nations, Locarno, Kellogg–Briand.

In August 1923, during the Ruhr occupation, President Ebert appointed Gustav Stresemann as his new chancellor and foreign secretary. Stresemann was forced to resign the chancellorship in November 1923, but remained as foreign secretary until 1929. During this time he was supported by moderate parties on both the right and left. This helped him to pass measures which brought recovery to the Weimar Republic.

First, Stresemann abolished the existing currency and set up a new one – the Rentenmark. Later, in 1924, a newly independent national bank, the Reichsbank, was given control of this currency. These changes increased confidence in Germany at home and abroad.

The Dawes Plan, 1924

In April 1924, Stresemann agreed the Dawes Plan. This addressed the reparations issue. Charles G. Dawes, an American banker, had been asked by the Allies to resolve Germany's non-payment. Under his plan:

- annual payments were reduced to an affordable level
- it was agreed that American banks would invest in German industry.

This combined package reassured the Allies that they would get their reparations payments. Stresemann had already called off passive resistance in the Ruhr by German workers. As a result, the French agreed to leave the Ruhr.

All this improved Germany's economy.

- Industrial output doubled during the period 1923-28, fuelled by US loans.
- Imports and exports increased.
- Employment went up.
- Government income from taxation improved.

Most Germans were reassured. However, there were drawbacks. The extreme political parties hated Treaty of Versailles and were furious that Germany had, again, agreed to pay reparations. Furthermore, the fragile economic recovery depended on American loans.

Source A: *a right-wing cartoon from 1923. A curtain is pulled back to reveal a fat American, with Jewish features, from Wall Street (the US financial centre). He is holding a rolled-up document called the Dawes Diktat. The caption says 'Here is your enemy'.*

The Young Plan, 1929

Stresemann made further progress with reparations five years later when, in the last year of his life, he agreed the Young Plan.

This plan was put forward in August 1929 by a committee, set up by the Allies, and headed by an American banker called Owen Young.

The Young Plan reduced the total reparations debt from £6.6 billion to £2 billion. Moreover, Germany was given a further 59 years to pay. This was a sensible measure.

- It reduced the annual amount the government had to pay.
- This made it possible to lower taxes.
- This, in turn, released spending power, which boosted German industry and employment.

Most saw this as a success for Stresemann. However, again there were drawbacks. The annual payments were still £50 million per year. Furthermore, they now stretched out until 1988. Several of the extreme political parties were incensed. The increasingly well-known leader of the Nazi Party, Adolf Hitler, said that extending the length of payments was 'passing on the penalty to the unborn'.

The Locarno Pact, 1925

Stresemann also made progress in international affairs. In October 1925 he signed the Locarno (or Rhineland) Pact. This was a treaty between Germany, Britain, France, Italy and Belgium.

- Germany agreed to keep its new 1919 border with France and Belgium.

In return:

- the last Allied troops left the Rhineland
- France promised peace with Germany
- the powers agreed to open talks about German membership of the **League of Nations**.

Stresemann saw this as a triumph; Germany was being treated as an equal, not dictated to. However, not all parties agreed; some resented the fact that the hated Versailles borders had been confirmed.

Source B: *a poster opposing the Young Plan, 1929. Germans are shown as slaves, shackled to work for the slave driver 'into the third generation' after Versailles.*

Activity

In the examination, most questions will require you to remember the key events in a topic. A mnemonic is a memory aid.

The main events of Stresemann's era were:

- his **C**urrency reform
- the **D**awes Plan
- the **Y**oung Plan
- the **L**ocarno Pact
- the **L**eague of Nations
- the **K**ellogg–Briand Pact.

Can you make a mnemonic using the highlighted initials? It could be a poem or a silly sentence – like **C**harlie, **D**o **Y**ou **L**ike **L**orraine **K**elly?

The League of Nations

At the end of the First World War, the Allies had founded the League of Nations. This was a new international body in which powerful countries discussed ways of solving the world's problems. But Germany had been excluded from membership. In September 1926, Stresemann persuaded the other great powers to accept Germany as a member. Germany was given a place on the League of Nations Council – which took the most important decisions of the League.

Not all political parties agreed that this was good. To some, the League was a symbol of the hated Treaty of Versailles. However, Stresemann's view was different. He saw it as another step towards German equality with other nations.

> …the League is the product of the treaties of 1919. Many disputes have arisen between the League and Germany because of these treaties. I hope that our co-operation with the League will make it easier in future to discuss these questions.

Source C: *extract from Stresemann's speech on German entry into the League of Nations in 1926.*

As a further sign of international approval for Germany, in 1926 Stresemann was awarded the Nobel Peace Prize.

Kellogg–Briand Pact

In August 1928, Germany became one of 62 countries to sign the Kellogg–Briand Pact – an international agreement in which states promised not to use war to achieve their foreign policy aims. It was not Stresemann's idea, but it was another sign that he had persuaded others to see Germany as a respectable member of the international community.

It was also one more thing to make moderate Germans feel that the Weimar Republic was becoming a success.

Source D: *a 1926 front page from the German magazine, Kladderadatsch. Germany lifts its Versailles tombstone, despite the efforts of the other great powers, and comes back from the dead.*

Activity

● As a class or a group, draw up a balance sheet of successes and failures for the Weimar Republic from 1923–29.

● Overall, how had it done?

● Compare your balance sheet with the one for page 17.

Between 1923 and 1929, moderate Germans regained confidence in the Weimar Republic. This confidence was reinforced in 1925 when Ebert, the president, was replaced by Paul von Hindenburg – the former field marshal of the Kaiser's army. Hindenburg seemed to give the Weimar Republic a strong **figurehead**.

- Stresemann had restored economic stability.
- He had also regained a place for Germany on the international stage.
- He had kept the support of moderate parties on the left and right.
- He was steering the Weimar Republic out of its troubled early years.

However, on 3 October 1929, Stresemann had a heart attack and died. The loss of his expertise and moderation was a severe blow to the Weimar Republic.

Worse still, later in October 1929, there was a world economic crisis and Germany was plunged back into unrest.

Source E: *a 1929 cartoon, entitled 'Tying Your Friend in Knots'. Briand (left), the French leader, greets Stresemann with a warm embrace – though he has taken care to make Germany powerless first. This illustrates the view of some Germans that France was not really treating Germany as an equal partner.*

ResultsPlus
Build Better Answers

Exam question: Describe the key features of the Stresemann era from 1923–29. **(6 marks)**
This question asks you to *select* and *communicate* information.

■ **A basic answer (level 1)** gives key features but without details (for example, *One feature of the Stresemann era was economic success*).

● **A good answer (level 2)** gives details to explain the key feature (for example, *One feature was economic success. German industrial output doubled between 1923 and 1928*).

▲ **An excellent answer (full marks)** gives three key features, each with details.

Economic crisis, 1929-32: the Great Depression

> ## Learning objectives
>
> In this chapter you will learn about:
> - the causes of the Great Depression in Germany
> - the effects of the Great Depression in Germany.

The Wall Street Crash

In October 1929, share prices began to fall on the Wall Street **stock exchange** in New York. Falling shares meant people's investments fell in value. Worried about losing money, people rushed to sell shares before they fell further. On 'Black Thursday', 24 October 1929, 13 million shares were sold. But this panic selling sent prices even lower. Shares worth $20,000 in the morning were worth $1000 by the end of the day's trading. Within a week, investors lost $4000 million. This is called the Wall Street Crash.

Economic effects

Banks were major investors in shares and suffered huge losses. German banks lost so much money that people feared they couldn't pay out the money in bank accounts. People rushed to get their money back – causing some banks to run out of cash.

Source A: *the collapse of the German Civil Servant Bank, 1929. People with bank accounts crowd around the locked doors, demanding their money back.*

All this spelt disaster for the German economy. German and American banks urgently needed the return of money they had lent to businesses. But German companies were dependent upon these loans. They either had to reduce operations or close. German industrial output fell and unemployment rose.

It was equally bad for companies that sold at home or abroad. The worldwide **depression** was a disaster for export industries but high unemployment meant that domestic demand for goods fell too. Unemployment rose further.

Years	Fall in industrial production (per cent)
1929–30	10%
1930–31	30%
1931–32	40%

Date	Unemployment
September 1929	1.3 million
September 1931	4.3 million
September 1932	5.1 million
January 1933	6.0 million

Source B: *a British cartoon from 1931. The banks suck their gold back into their reserves; money for European industry dries up.*

Social and political effects

The economic collapse caused suffering.

- The middle classes lost savings, their companies or their homes.
- Workers became unemployed.

People demanded political action, but the Weimar government failed them. From 1930 to 1932, the chancellor was Heinrich Brüning. He proposed:

- raising taxes to pay the cost of unemployment benefit
- reducing unemployment benefit to make payments more affordable.

This pleased no one. Right-wing parties, the middle classes and the wealthy opposed higher taxes. Left-wing parties and the working classes opposed lower benefits. The coalition of parties which Brüning's government depended upon collapsed in 1930. Brüning could only govern by decree. There had only been five presidential decrees in 1930. As the crisis deepened, Brüning's government had to rely on 44 decrees in 1931 and 66 in 1932.

But even this was in vain – the causes of suffering were beyond government control and the crisis continued. Useless decrees merely undermined confidence in the Weimar Republic still further.

The unemployed roamed the streets; some joined the private armies of political parties. Violent clashes became common. Brüning had lost control of the Reichstag, the economy and the streets. He resigned in 1932, leaving a dangerous **power vacuum** for a new leader to step into.

Four private armies, with knives, revolvers and knuckle-dusters rampaged through towns – the SA of the Nazis, the Red Front of the KPD the Sozi of the SPD and the Stahlhelmer. The Reichswehr (the army) were nowhere.

Source C: *Kurt Ludecke, an eyewitness, reporting in 1930.*

ResultsPlus
Build Better Answers

Exam question: Explain the effects of the Great Depression in Germany. (8 marks)

■ **A basic answer (level 1)** gives an effect (for example, *the public suffered*) but no detail.

● **A good answer (level 2)** gives details about the effects (for example, by stating *the public suffered* and then going on to give figures for job losses).

▲ **A better answer (level 3)** gives at least two effects (for example, economic, social and/or political) and explains how they came about.

▲ **An excellent answer (full marks)** links them (for example, showing that a consequence of the Depression was high unemployment and linking that to violence in the streets and a loss of trust in the Weimar government).

Source D: *a 1950s painting showing the unemployed and beggars outside a closed German factory in the Great Depression.*

Activity

Make a list of the effects of the Great Depression in Germany. Write each effect on a card.

1 Organise the cards into economic, social and political effects.
2 Some of the effects are linked, for example unemployment was linked to political unrest. What other links can you find?

In the Unit 2 exam, you will be required to answer questions on one country. You will have to answer six questions: Question 1 (a), (b), (c) and (d); either Question 2 (a) or Question 2 (b); and either Question 3 (a) or Question 3 (b).

You only have an hour and 15 minutes to answer these questions. The number of marks available for each question helps you judge how long to spend on each answer, but as a guide you might consider allocating your time as follows:

Question 1 (a)   6 minutes   Question 1 (b)   8 minutes   Question 1 (c)   12 minutes
Question 1 (d)   12 minutes   Question 2   12 minutes   Question 3   25 minutes

Remember to leave a few minutes at the end to check your spelling, punctuation and grammar in your answers to questions 2 and 3. Here we are going to look at Question 1 (a) and (b).

ResultsPlus
Build Better Answers

Question 1 (a)

Tip: Question 1 (a) will ask you to make an inference from a source and provide evidence from the source to support it. Let's look at an example. On page 13 you are told:
In August 1923, a new chancellor was appointed – Gustav Stresemann. In November 1923, he cancelled the old mark and issued a new currency – the Rentenmark. This led to a period of stability.
A suitable question for this source would be:

What can you learn from this source about Germany in 1923? (4 marks)

Student answer	Examiner comments
This source tells me that Stresemann was appointed in 1923 and that he introduced a new currency, the Rentenmark. It also tells me that he took over a country that had many problems.	The first part of this answer merely repeats information contained in the source, so it would be marked in the bottom level. The last sentence does make an inference (a judgment which is not actually stated in the source) when it says that the country had many problems. But it does not say what in the source makes it possible to make that inference.

Let's rewrite the answer with that additional detail.

| This source tells me that Stresemann was appointed in 1923 and that he introduced a new currency, the Rentenmark. It also tells me that he took over a country that had many problems. I know this because he had to cancel the old currency and introduce a new one. You don't do serious things like that unless there is a real problem. It also says it led to stability – so that proves that before there must have been instability. | An inference is made and two pieces of support are given; this is enough for 4 marks. |

ResultsPlus
Build Better Answers

Question 1 (b)

Tip: Question 1 (b) will ask you to explain the key features of an event you are studying. Sometimes the words 'key features' will actually appear in the question. Or you could be asked about problems, policies or effects. Don't just tell the story. Think about the information and organise it as if you were putting it under headings. This type of question requires you to write at greater length than Question 1 (a) and is worth 6 marks. Let's look at an example.

Describe the effects of the Treaty of Versailles on Germany. (6 marks)

Student answer	Examiner comments
The effects on Germany were very serious. There were limitations on the armed forces, land was taken away and Germany had to pay compensation for the losses during the war.	This is an unusual answer because it has done the hard work without doing the easy bit! It would be very easy to just list the terms of the treaty and not find the 'headings' under which to put them. This answer has done the opposite. It has listed three features to write about, but has given no detail. That would keep it in Level 1 for making just 'simple statements'.

Let's rewrite the answer with the detail added.

The effects on Germany were very serious. There were limitations on the armed forces. The German army was reduced to 100,000 men and Germany was forbidden to have tanks or submarines. Land was taken away and Germany lost all its colonies, which were to be administered by other powers under League of Nations control. It had to give Alsace and Lorraine back to France. It also had to pay compensation for the losses during the war – these were reparations. No figure was agreed at Versailles, but later it was fixed at £6600 million.	Very nice. Three features supported. There is always more detail that could be provided, but this is sufficient to score full marks in Level 2 for 'developed statements'.

Key Topic 2: Hitler and the growth of the Nazi Party 1918-33

Adolf Hitler was born in Braunau, in Austria, on 20 April 1889. He was, therefore, an Austrian, not a German. Hitler's father was an Austrian customs official, who beat him violently as a boy. Despite all this, Adolf Hitler rose to become the leader of Germany.

In this Key Topic, you will study:

○ The founding and early growth of the Nazi Party, 1919–23
○ The Munich Putsch and the lean years, 1923–29
○ Increased support and political developments, 1929–January 1933

Adolf Hitler – early life

Learning objectives

In this chapter you will learn about:

● Hitler's youth in Austria
● Hitler's move to Germany and service in the First World War
● Hitler's first political activity.

At school, Hitler loved the history, literature and music of the Germanic people. Above all, he dreamed of a future as a great artist or an architect. But he did badly in exams and failed to gain a place at an art academy. He became a rebel. School friends remembered his passionate beliefs.

> His speeches seemed to be like a volcano erupting. It was as though something quite apart from him was bursting out...I was astonished at how fluently he expressed himself.

Source B: *August Kubizek, describing his 16-year-old friend Adolf Hitler.*

Source A: *Hitler, aged 16, drawn by a school friend.*

After leaving school, Hitler worked as a sign writer, a house painter, even a road sweeper in Vienna, Austria's capital. At times a virtual tramp, he was embittered by this early lack of success. He followed local politics. Vienna had a strongly anti-Jewish mayor at this time, named Karl Lueger. Hitler began to blame the Jews for dominating industry and the art world, and reducing chances for people like him.

Hitler and the First World War

In 1913, Hitler went to Munich, a city in Bavaria, in the south of Germany. He arrived there with one small bag, to study art. But then the First World War broke out.

Hitler was filled with joy. He saw war as a chance to unite all the Germanic people of Europe. Hitler joined the German Army. He served in the 16th Bavarian Infantry Regiment in France and saw harsh times. Out of 3600 men in his regiment, only 611 survived the first week. But Hitler was a good soldier. He became a corporal and was awarded the Iron Cross (First Class) for bravery. Wartime boosted his confidence. He called it 'the most memorable period of my life'.

German defeat was a blow to Hitler. He had been wounded by gas and heard the news in hospital. He railed against the 'traitors' who had 'betrayed' Germany by accepting peace. He believed that the German Army had not been defeated; it had been 'stabbed in the back' by socialists and Jews.

After the war

After the war, Hitler was given an army assignment checking up on political groups. One of these was the German Workers' Party (DAP), a small group founded on 5 January 1919 by Anton Drexler. Hitler attended two meetings in September 1919; there were only 23 people present at the first meeting and 40 at the second.

Eventually, Hitler joined this group – becoming its seventh committee member – and turned it into the Nazi Party. Within 15 years, the Nazi Party would be the biggest political party in Germany – and Adolf Hitler the German leader.

> I want to call to account the November Criminals of 1918. It cannot be that two million Germans have fallen in vain. We demand revenge.

Source C: *Hitler in a later speech.*

> There was no way to compromise with the Jews. For my part, I decided right then that I would take up political work.

Source D: *Hitler, in his book* Mein Kampf, *1925–26.*

Examination question

Describe Hitler's views about the Treaty of Versailles. **(6 marks)**

Tip: This is a '*selection* and *communication* of information' question. There will always be one of these in your examination paper.

There is a similar question on page 11. Use the advice for that question to organise your answer to this one.

Did you know?

Hitler's father was originally named Alois Schicklgruber. He was 39 years old when he took the name Hitler, before Adolf was born. Perhaps it was a good thing for Hitler. 'Heil Schicklgruber' hasn't the same ring about it!

Source E: *Hitler (right) in 1914, during the First World War.*

The birth of the Nazi Party, 1919-23

> ### Learning objectives
>
> In this chapter you will learn about:
> - the German Workers' Party (DAP) when Hitler joined
> - the early Nazi Party, its aims and early features, including the SA.

At first, the DAP was only a small and little-known group. In the autumn of 1919, when Hitler joined, it had about 40 regular members. At Hitler's third meeting, the treasurer announced its entire funds – 7 marks and 50 pfennig. But Hitler shared the party's main views. They railed against:

- the communists and socialists, whom they blamed for bringing down the Kaiser
- the Weimar politicians who had accepted the Treaty of Versailles
- the weakness of all democracies
- the Jews, whom they blamed for undermining the German economy.

Source A: 'In the beginning, there was the word' – a 1937 painting by Hermann Hoyer, showing Hitler addressing the early Nazi Party in 1921.

The 25-Point Programme

By 1920, Hitler was working as Drexler's right-hand man. In February 1920, the two men revealed the new 25-Point Programme of the DAP. This included:

- scrapping the Treaty of Versailles
- expanding Germany's borders to give its people lebensraum – more land to live in
- depriving the Jews of German citizenship.

The programme also made clear that the DAP were willing to use force to achieve all this.

Hitler was an energetic, passionate speaker and his public speaking started to attract larger numbers to meetings. Many people were dissatisfied with the Weimar Republic in the period up to 1923, and Hitler's group attracted supporters from the army, the police and small businesses. Membership grew rapidly, to about 1100 in June 1920.

> The man…knew how to fire up people – not with arguments, impossible in hate speeches – but with the fanaticism of his manner, screaming and yelling, and by deafening repetition, and contagious rhythm. It has a fearfully exciting primitive and barbaric effect.

Source B: Carl Suckmayer, who heard Hitler in Munich beer halls in 1923. He said he was so close, he could see spit flying from under his moustache.

Activity

As you read through this chapter:

- list the types of people that were attracted to the DAP
- list the views and policies that attracted them to the DAP.

Hitler's role grows

On 7 August 1920, at Hitler's suggestion, the DAP changed its name to the National Socialist German Workers' Party (NSDAP, or Nazi Party for short). The party then adopted the swastika as its emblem, and its members began to use the raised arm salute. Membership increased to 3000 during 1920. Increased membership boosted funds and the party was able to buy a newspaper – the *Völkischer Beobachter* – for 180,000 marks, enabling it to spread its views even further.

In mid-1921, Hitler pushed Drexler aside and became the party Führer, or leader. He gathered around him loyal party leaders:

- Ernst Röhm, a scar-faced, bull-necked soldier
- Hermann Goering, a wealthy hero of the German Air Force
- Rudolf Hess, a wealthy academic who became Hitler's deputy
- Julius Streicher, founder of another Nazi paper, *Der Stürmer*.

Hitler also cultivated powerful friends, such as General Ludendorff, leader of the German Army during the First World War.

In 1921, Hitler created the **Sturmabteilung** (SA), or storm troopers. These were the party's private army. They were recruited from demobilised soldiers, (ones no longer serving) the unemployed and students. These 'Brownshirts' provided security at meetings and bodyguards for Nazi leaders; they also broke up meetings of opposition groups. Hitler put Röhm in charge of the SA. Many of the SA were thugs and difficult to control, so in 1923 Hitler selected trusted members of the SA and formed his own bodyguard, the Stosstrupp or Shock Troop.

In 1923, Hitler was an unlikely future ruler of Germany. His control of the NSDAP was shaky. Furthermore, it was only one of many right-wing groups in Germany. It had no seats in the Reichstag and was mainly confined to Bavaria, in southern Germany. But with his loyal lieutenants and SA thugs, Hitler had the nucleus of the party that would later take him to power.

> Hitler's army supporters, tough as leather and hard as Krupp steel, eagerly went into battle armed with rubber truncheons and riding whips. Troublemakers were hustled away, order was restored and Hitler resumed speaking.

Source C: *DAP meeting in 1920, described in* Adolf Hitler *by John Toland, 1976.*

ResultsPlus
Build Better Answers

Exam question: Study Source C What can you learn from Source C about troublemakers at Hitler's meetings? (4 marks)

This is an *inference* question. It asks you to work something out from the source.

■ **A basic answer (level 1)** gives information from the source (for example, *troublemakers were hustled away*).

● **A good answer (level 2)** makes an inference (for example, *people wanting to cause trouble at Hitler's meetings had little chance of success*) but without supporting it from the source.

▲ **An excellent answer (full marks)** uses details from the source to support that inference (for example, by adding *because Hitler had a tough group of army supporters, with the strength and the weapons to make sure that opponents were removed*).

Source D: *Social Democrats noticed the threat of the NSDAP. This SPD poster from 1922 says 'Your enemy is on the Right' and shows an SA trooper, complete with brown uniform and swastika.*

The Munich Putsch, 1923

Learning objectives

In this chapter you will learn about:

● the causes, events and results of the Munich Putsch.

Activity

'The Munich Putsch did not succeed, but it was not a failure.'

● As you go through this chapter, draw up a balance sheet, noting down Hitler's successes and failures during the Munich Putsch.

● At the end, decide whether you agree or disagree with the statement above.

Causes

In November 1923, Hitler launched the Munich Putsch – an uprising against the German government. He had three reasons for doing so.

● Firstly, hyperinflation was making the lives of Germans miserable. The French occupation of the Ruhr had also angered them. Hitler wanted to exploit this discontent. Membership of the NSDAP had grown to about 55,000, mainly people from around Munich, the capital of Bavaria, in the south of Germany. This was Hitler's chance to make an impact nationally.

● Secondly, Hitler sensed that the new government of Gustav Stresemann would soon get on top of Germany's economic and international problems. He needed to act before unrest died down.

● Thirdly, Stresemann's government was starting to crack down on extremist groups. The army had recently put down a left-wing revolt in Saxony. Hitler could see a crackdown on right-wing groups coming next.

Events

On the evening of 8 November 1923, there was a meeting of 3000 officials of the Bavarian government in a beer hall, called the Burgerbrau Keller, in Munich. The three main speakers were von Kahr, the leader of the Bavarian government, von Seisser, the head of the Bavarian police, and von Lossow, the head of the army in Bavaria.

Hitler burst in, with 600 SA storm troopers, brandishing a gun. He released a shot into the ceiling and announced that he was taking over the government of Bavaria. He claimed that, after taking control in Munich, he would then march against the German government itself. He was supported by the famous German general, Erich von Ludendorff. Kahr, Seisser and Lossow were taken off into a side room. Confronted with Hitler, his troops and their weapons, they agreed to support the uprising.

However, the next morning, Hitler heard that Kahr, Seisser and Lossow had changed their minds and opposed him. This was a blow. The SA had only 2000 rifles, far fewer than the local police and army forces, but Hitler pressed on. He sent 3000 supporters to key buildings around the town, each group supported by the SA.

Source A: *the front of this magazine from 1924 shows Kahr carrying Hitler into attack, but also summoning soldiers to arrest him.*

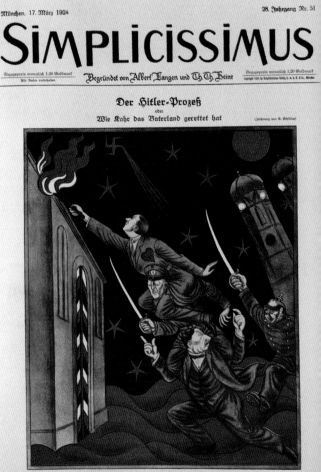

Hitler, his key supporters and his Shock Troop marched on the town centre to declare him the president of Germany. But, in a narrow street called Residenzstrasse, they were met by state police, who opened fire. A bodyguard, Graf, threw himself in front of Hitler and was hit by several bullets. Goering fell, shot in the thigh. Hitler was dragged to the ground by his bodyguards with such force that his left arm was dislocated. In all, 14 of Hitler's supporters and four police were killed.

Ludendorff was arrested. Other rebels fled; one group entered a nearby ladies' academy and hid under the beds. Hitler fled the scene in a car. He hid at the house of a friend, ten miles south of Munich, but was later found and arrested.

Results

Hitler and several other leaders of the Putsch were put on trial. He was found guilty of **treason** and sentenced to five years in gaol at Landsberg Castle. The NSDAP was banned. In the short term, the Munich Putsch was therefore a defeat and a humiliation for Hitler.

However, it could have been worse. The judge was quite lenient – five years was the minimum sentence allowed for treason. Ludendorff, incredibly, was even found not guilty. Furthermore, in the longer term, the results were not all bad.

- Hitler used his trial to get national publicity for his views.
- The ban on the NSDAP was weakly enforced and then lifted in 1925. As a result of the publicity, the NSDAP won its first seats in the Reichstag – 32 seats in the May 1924 election.
- Hitler was released after only nine months.
- Hitler used his time in gaol to write his autobiography – *Mein Kampf (My Struggle)*. It contained his political ideas and became the guiding light of the Nazi Party.
- Finally, Hitler realised he needed a new approach to gain power in Germany (see below).

Source B: *a group of Hitler's Stosstrupp (Shock Troop), in Munich on the morning of the Putsch.*

Examination question

Describe the key features of the Munich Putsch. (6 marks)

ResultsPlus
Top Tip

The above question is about *key features*. Students who do well in these questions organise their information.

You need to make sure you identify a key feature and then provide information about it. For example, what information would you give about:

- the failure of the Putsch on the day
- the longer-term results?

There was a key features question on page 21. Use the advice there to help you here.

Instead of an armed coup, we shall have to hold our noses and enter the Reichstag…If outvoting them takes longer than outshooting them, at least the result will be guaranteed…Sooner or later we shall have a majority and, after that – Germany!

Source C: *from a letter written by Hitler from gaol. The strategy he describes did later get him into power.*

Did you know?

Hitler spent two days hiding in the attic at his friend's house after the failure of the Munich Putsch. The family gardener informed police and Hitler was arrested after he was found hiding in a wardrobe.

The rebirth of Nazism, 1924

Learning objectives

In this chapter you will learn about:

● the political ideas of the Nazi Party after 1924, including:

  ▪ nationalism, socialism and totalitarianism

  ▪ traditional German values, struggle and 'racial purity'.

Activity

As you read this chapter, think about this task.

Using the sources in this chapter and on other pages in this book, write two lists, showing:

● what Nazi posters supported

● what Nazi posters criticised.

Hitler left prison in 1924 with a clearer vision for his Nazi Party. Some ideas were shared with other parties; some were his own. There are several places where we can see what Hitler's Nazi Party stood for:

● *Mein Kampf*, Hitler's **blueprint** for the party

● *The Second Book* or *Secret Book*, which Hitler wrote in 1928, though it was not published until 1959, well after he died

● Hitler's speeches, publications and actions.

From these, it is clear that National Socialism, or Nazism, had key features.

Nationalism

This involved:

● breaking the restrictions on Germany in the Treaty of Versailles

● reviving the power of Germany

● making Germany self-sufficient, not dependent on imports from abroad (autarky)

● expanding Germany's borders

● purifying the German 'race'.

Socialism

● Like the communists, Hitler wanted to control big businesses.

● However, communists wanted to place all private land and businesses in the hands of the workers. Hitler did not support this form of socialism.

● To him, socialism meant running the economy in the national interest so that:

  ● both agriculture and industry would flourish

  ● businesses would not make unfair profits

  ● Jews could not control businesses

  ● workers would be treated fairly.

Source A: *a 1924 Nazi Party poster. The businessman, clearly Jewish, his factories smoking in the background, has the despairing German people at his feet, tethered like puppets.*

The National Government will save the farmer – and secure the nation's food supply – and save the worker by a massive attack on unemployment. Standing above classes, it will bring political unity to the people.

Source B: *from the 1933 Nazi Party manifesto.*

Totalitarianism

This was the belief that the Nazi Party should *totally* control every aspect of life.

- Hitler despised democracy. He said it was weak.
- He believed in the Führerprinzip (leadership principle); total loyalty to the leader. This way, he said, the leader could organise every aspect of society for the benefit of the German people.

Traditional German values

Hitler said that moral and cultural values had been weakened in the Weimar Republic. He wanted the return of:

- strong family values, with clear male and female roles
- Christian morality
- old-style German culture, with traditional art, music and theatre.

> We shall take Christianity as the basis for our morality and the family as the nucleus of our nation and state.

Source C: *from the 1933 Nazi Party manifesto.*

Struggle

Hitler believed that life was a contest, in which people constantly struggled against each other. He said that this constant struggle made people and countries healthier and fitter. Nazis believed that Germany should struggle:

- outside her borders, against other countries, for land – to get lebensraum (living space), so that all German people could live together, united
- inside her borders, against non-German people, so that they could strengthen the true German race.

Racial purity

Hitler said that people were divided into superior and inferior races.

- According to Hitler, the Aryans were the superior race. These were the Germanic people of northern Europe, who, he said, had produced all that was good in human culture.
- He believed that other races, from places like eastern Europe (for example, the Slavs), and from Asia and Africa, were inferior races.
- The lowest form of life, he said, were the Jews, whom he described as parasites who fed off the countries they lived in.

Source D: *a Nazi poster from 1924 showing the combination of dominant working man and the woman as the mother figure – both of them serving the national flag.*

Examination question

Describe the key features of National Socialism. **(6 marks)**

Tip: There may well be a question asking for *key features* in your examination. There was a key features question on page 21. Use the advice there to help you here.

Nazi Party organisation in the lean years, 1924–29

> ### Learning objectives
>
> In this chapter you will learn about:
> - how Hitler improved the organisation and finance of the NSDAP
> - the growth of the SA; the start of the SS
> - Joseph Goebbels and Nazi propaganda
> - weak Nazi results in national elections, 1924–29.

Hitler re-launched the Nazi Party on 27 February 1925 – ironically at the Burgerbrau Keller, scene of the Munich Putsch. He had lost none of his personal appeal: 4000 people heard him speak; a further 1000 had to be turned away.

Hitler appointed two efficient organisers to run Nazi headquarters: Philipp Bouhler as secretary and Franz Schwarz as treasurer. He also divided the party into regions and appointed a network of gauleiters answerable only to him, who ran the NSDAP in each gaue, or region.

To fund all this, Hitler improved party finances. He befriended Germany's most wealthy businessmen. They shared his hatred of communism and hoped Hitler would limit the power of trade unions. By the early 1930s, the Nazis were receiving donations from giants of German industry, such as Thyssen, Krupp and Bosch.

This extra income also helped Hitler to expand the SA. It had 400,000 members by 1930. The Munich Putsch had taught Hitler the importance of a totally loyal bodyguard but Hitler didn't trust the SA. Many storm troopers were violent thugs and difficult to control, and while Hitler was in prison the SA had developed a dangerous loyalty to Ernst Röhm, its commander. So, in 1925, Hitler set up a new party security group. He called them the **Schutzstaffel** (Protection Squad), or SS.

At first, the SS was run by Hitler's personal chauffeur and bodyguard, Julius Schreck, and soon after by Heinrich Himmler, one of his most loyal supporters. The SS became famous – and feared – for their menacing black uniforms (introduced in 1932).

Hitler also worked with Dr Joseph Goebbels to improve Nazi party propaganda. Propaganda is the information or the ideas that you spread to help your own cause or harm other people's. Hitler and Goebbels had a simple message, but they created many ways to get it across.

Activity

Be the author! This chapter has a main heading but it has no subheadings.

Put yourself in the place of the author. As you read this chapter, choose subheadings that would point out to the reader the *key features of Nazi Party organisation, 1924–29*. For example, you could start with 'Re-launch'.

There may well be an examination question asking you for the key features of a topic – so this is good practice.

Source A: *the Schutzstaffel, or SS, parading in 1933.*

- They created scapegoats whom they blamed for Germany's problems: the Jews, the communists and the moderate leaders of the Weimar Republic – especially the Social Democrats, who had signed the Armistice and Treaty of Versailles.
- They promoted Hitler as the voice of the Nazi Party. By the 1930s, his speeches were reported in 120 daily or weekly Nazi newspapers, read by hundreds of thousands of Germans across the whole country.
- They used the most up-to-date technology, including radio, films and gramophone records, to keep Hitler in the public eye. Hitler used aeroplanes to fly from venue to venue, so that he could speak in up to five cities a day.
- They created a clear image for the party – an image of strength. The image was set by Hitler's passion, the spectacle of mass Nazi **rallies** and the impressive power of the SA.

By 1929, the Nazi Party was well organised. It had 100,000 members and Hitler was a national figure. However, in some ways, these were lean years.

- Since 1923, inflation had eased, employment had increased and the public were better off.
- Stresemann seemed to be regaining status for Germany on the world stage.
- In 1925, Hindenburg, the 78-year-old ex-field marshal of the German Army, had become president; his reputation made more people support the Weimar Republic.

As a result, voters supported moderate parties, such as the socialists, and all the extreme parties lost ground. In the **general elections** of May 1928:

- the Nazis won only 12 seats
- they were the ninth biggest Reichstag party
- they polled only 810,000 votes – just 2.6% of the national vote.

A numerically insignificant...radical-revolutionary splinter group incapable of exerting any noticeable influence on the great mass of the people and the course of political events.

Source C: *a confidential report on the Nazis by the Interior Ministry, July 1927.*

Propaganda must confine itself to very few points and repeat them endlessly. Here, persistence is the first and foremost condition of success.

Source B: *Hitler, writing in* Mein Kampf.

ResultsPlus
Build Better Answers

Exam question: Explain how Hitler changed the Nazi Party between 1924 and 1929. **(8 marks)**

This question requires an *explanation of change*. It is not enough to describe what happened to the Nazi Party in these years. You will need to give examples of ways in which these things made a difference to the Party.

■ **A basic answer (level 1)** gives an example of a change, but without details (for example, *Hitler improved Nazi Party finances*).

● **A good answer (level 2)** provides details about the examples (for example, gives details of the donations received from wealthy businessmen).

▲ **A better answer (level 3)** explains at least two changes, showing what difference they made to the Nazi party (for example, adds *the improvement in party finances meant that the Nazis could afford to distribute its propaganda and run expensive political campaigns. Hitler could use aeroplanes to fly from venue to venue*).

▲ **An excellent answer (full marks)** links the changes.

ResultsPlus
Top Tip

When answering *change* questions, students often just list the changes – with a series of sentences, one sentence about each change. This kind of answer sets out the changes like washing on a line, each change hanging there separately.

However, students who do well will set out the changes more like a jigsaw. They *link* the changes, to show that they were not separate. For example: *One change in the Nazi Party was that Hitler got more money for the party.* (Give detail to show how.) *This change was linked to another change. The extra money meant that the Nazi Party could afford to be much better organised.* (Give details to show how.)

Nazi support grows, 1929-32

> **Learning objectives**
>
> In this chapter you will learn about:
> - how much the support for the Nazis grew, 1929–32
> - why support for the Nazis grew, 1929–32
> - who supported the Nazis, 1929–32.

Nazi support grows

In October 1929, share prices crashed on Wall Street, the US stock exchange (see pages 22–23). American banks recalled loans to German industries and banks, causing many to close. Unemployment rose and savings were lost, bringing suffering to working people and the middle classes alike. Unrest increased as people demonstrated in the streets.

Chancellor Brüning could not get majority support in the Reichstag and had to govern by presidential decree. He tried raising taxes to pay benefits to the poor. He tried banning demonstrations to calm unrest. All failed. Voters turned to the extreme right-wing and left-wing parties to solve their problems.

General elections 1928–32: seats in the Reichstag and votes

	May 1928	**Sept 1930**	**July 1932**
National Socialists	12 seats	107 seats	230 seats
Communists	54 seats	77 seats	89 seats
The Nazi vote	1 million	6 million	13 million

Hitler's appeal

Hitler was one of the reasons people turned to the Nazis. He was the party's **figurehead**. He appeared everywhere. He used aeroplanes in a whirlwind campaign for the 1930 and 1932 elections. Germans saw him as man who could:

- be a strong leader
- unite the country
- restore order from social unrest
- force other nations to scrap the Treaty of Versailles
- persuade other nations to treat Germany fairly.

Since the First World War, Germany's national pride had suffered. Promises to 'tear up the Treaty of Versailles' and restore social order were very popular with the German people.

Source A: *this 1931 Nazi cartoon shows Brüning sitting in government on a throne propped up by new taxes, bans and Article 48 decrees.*

> Goebbels organised 6000 meetings in halls and huge tents that could hold 10,000 and in the open air. Never had Germany been subjected to such persuasion.

Source B: *description of the 1930 elections from* Adolf Hitler *by John Toland, 1976.*

> **Activity**
>
> Between 1928 and 1933:
> - unemployment rose from 1 million to 5 million
> - Nazi votes in general elections rose from 1 million to 13 million.
>
> How might these changes be linked?

The strength of the SA

The main opponent for the NSDAP was the Communist Party. One factor in the electoral success of the NSDAP was that it had a stronger private army than the communists. By 1930, the SA had 400,000 brown-shirted storm troopers.

- Firstly, the SA was used in rallies to make the Nazi Party seem strong, organised, disciplined and reliable. In the midst of economic and social turmoil, the Nazis seemed strong enough to control unrest and stand up to foreign powers.

- Secondly, the SA storm troopers were used to whip up feelings of hope for the future.

> It was 10 pm when the first torchlight appeared. Then 2000 brown shirts followed like waves in the sea. Their faces shone with energy in the light of the torches. It was a magnificent picture…boots and gauntlets, swords, flags…We were drunk with enthusiasm.

Source D: *Frau Solmitz, a middle-class lady, writing in her diary for February 1933.*

- Finally, these Nazi storm troopers were used to disrupt opposition parties. The elections of 1930 and 1932 were violent. Armed, uniformed men tore down opposition posters, intimidated their candidates, broke into their offices and disrupted their rallies. In 1932, in one clash alone in Hamburg, 19 people were killed. Voters were also intimidated outside polling stations.

Working-class support

The Nazis had different appeal for different people.

- Many working people were attracted by Nazi support for traditional German values and a strong Germany.

- The Nazis promised them 'Work and Bread' on posters.

- They also used posters which gave the impression that working people supported the Nazis. After all, they were originally called the German Workers' Party.

The working class were important in politics. They were the biggest group of voters. But the NSDAP never dominated the working-class vote. When times were hard, many workers supported the communists, so Nazi working-class support was important; but it wasn't enough.

> It must have been in 1930 or 1931 that my mother saw an SA parade in the streets of Heidelberg. Discipline in a time of chaos…won her over. Without ever having read a pamphlet, she joined the party.

Source C: *from* Inside the Third Reich: Memoirs, *Albert Speer, 1970.*

Source E: *a 1950s painting showing a lorry full of Nazi storm troopers driving through a communist rally outside the KPD headquarters.*

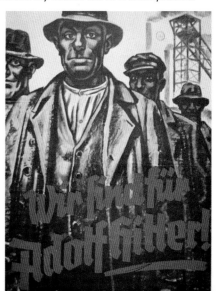

Source F: *a NSDAP poster from 1934 showing strong, determined industrial workers and the words 'We support Adolf Hitler'.*

Middle-class support

One key group in the growth of Nazi support was the middle class, which contained professional people, like teachers and lawyers, business people and small farmers. They often owned land or businesses and had savings. Between 1929 and 1932, they deserted the moderate parties, like the Social Democrats and the German People's Party, and supported the Nazis. There were several reasons for this.

- The Great Depression had hurt the middle classes. Many had lost their companies, their savings or their pensions. They saw Hitler as a strong leader who could help the country recover.
- They were also afraid of the growing Communist Party after 1929. The communists wanted to abolish private ownership of land and businesses. The middle classes saw the Nazis as a strong party which could protect them from the communists.
- There was also a view that there had been a moral decline under the Weimar Republic, including more drinking and sexual openness. The Nazis represented a return to traditional German values. This went down well with the middle classes.

Farmers

The Nazis targeted farmers in particular. The Nazi policy of confiscating all private land (in the 25 Points of 1920) was changed in 1928. The new policy said that private land would only be confiscated if owned by Jews. So Hitler could promise to protect the farmers from the Communist Party, which would have confiscated their land.

Big business

The support of big business was another reason for the growth of the Nazi the Party after 1929. The wealthy business classes usually supported the National Party. But this party, along with the more moderate parties, declined after 1929 – its Reichstag seats were cut by half. Industrialists saw Hitler as their best hope of protection from the rise of the communists.

There were two main benefits from this for the Nazis.

- Nazi finances benefited from wealthy businessmen, like Benz and Krupps, who began to pour money into the NSDAP.
- Nazi propaganda benefited too. The National Party leader, Alfred Hugenberg, was a newspaper tycoon. He allowed Goebbels to use his newspapers for Nazi propaganda against the communists.

> The German farmer stands between two great dangers today – one is the American capitalist system and the other is the Marxist system of the Bolsheviks. Who alone can save the farmer from these dangers? NATIONAL SOCIALISM

Source G: *extract from a Nazi election leaflet of 1932.*

Source H: *a cartoon from 1929, showing Hitler being given a leg-up by Hugenberg, the leader of the National Party.*

Young people and women

The Nazi Party also gained support from women and the young.

- Young people were attracted by Hitler's passionate speeches, his ambitions for the future and the atmosphere of Nazi rallies.
- At first, women did not support the Nazis, whose policies towards women restricted them. However, Nazi propaganda made special appeals to women. It claimed that voting for the NSDAP was best for their country and best for their families.

Something for everyone

No single group was the key to Nazi success. Some historians say this was new for German politics and helped the NSDAP to grow.

> We do not recognise classes. The German people, with its millions of farmers, citizens and workers, will, together, overcome distress.

Source J: *Hitler in a speech in January 1933.*

> In 1930, he was offering something new to Germans – unity. He welcomed all. There was no class distinction; the only demand was to follow Hitler in his fight against Jews and Reds, in his struggle for Lebensraum and the glory and good of Germany.

Source K: *extract from* Adolf Hitler *by John Toland, 1976.*

Therefore, between 1929 and 1932, the Nazis grew from what the Interior Ministry called an 'insignificant' threat to the biggest party in the Reichstag, with 230 members. Moderate members cringed in the Reichstag as the Nazi delegates answered to the initial roll call with 'Present. Heil Hitler!'

> This was the elite of the Aryan race! This noisy, shouting uniformed gang…with the faces of criminals and degenerates.

Source L: *Toni Sender, who was an SPD member of the Reichstag in 1932.*

Nazi progress would not stop here. There was more to come in 1933.

Source I: *a Nazi poster from 1932. It appeals to women to look after their children's future and their demoralised husbands by voting for Hitler.*

ResultsPlus
Build Better Answers

Exam question: Was the Great Depression the main reason why the Nazi Party grew between 1929 and 1932? Explain your answer.
You may use the following to help you:
- **the Great Depression**
- **Nazi propaganda**
- **the communist threat**
- **the strength of the SA.**
(16 marks)

Remember that there are additional marks for spelling, punctuation and grammar for this question.

A good answer (level 2) gives details about one or more reasons (for example, details of unemployment during the Depression).

A better answer (level 3) considers several reasons and decides whether one reason was the main cause. If there is a main cause, the answer would justify that choice.

An excellent answer (level 4) explains why some reasons were more important, but also sees that these were linked to other reasons. (For example: *The Great Depression was the most important reason because it caused suffering, which made the working people and middle classes desert the moderate parties. But Nazi propaganda was also vital. Without all that, the public would still have deserted the moderate parties, but they could have voted for someone else, like the communists*).

The Nazis win power, 1932-33

Learning objectives

In this chapter you will learn about:

- Hitler standing for election as president
- a series of chancellors falling from power
- Hitler becoming chancellor in January 1933.

By July 1932, the NSDAP was the biggest party in the Reichstag. Meanwhile, Hitler had been trying to increase his *personal* power. In March 1932, he stood as a candidate in the **presidential elections**.

The presidential elections of 1932

Germany was in turmoil at this time. The Wall Street Crash had caused the collapse of German industry and banking. Unemployment and the loss of savings caused hardship and unrest. As in the general elections, people protested by voting for extreme candidates. Hindenburg, president since 1925, hung on with 18 million votes. The Communist leader, Ernst Thällmann, polled only 5 million. However, Hitler polled 11 million votes.

Because no candidate had achieved 50 per cent of the vote, the election was repeated in April. Hindenburg polled 19 million and was re-elected president. However, while the Communist vote fell to 4 million, Hitler's vote grew to 13 million. Hitler was now a major political figure in Germany.

The fall of Chancellor Brüning

In April 1932, the moderate socialist chancellor, Brüning, used a presidential decree to ban the SA and SS. He wanted to calm unrest and control the Nazis. But right-wing parties were angered. An ambitious general, Kurt von Schleicher, decided to remove Brüning. He organised a coalition of right-wing groups, consisting of landowners, industrialists and army officers. Then he persuaded Hindenburg that they had a majority in the Reichstag, and Brüning was sacked.

Von Papen becomes chancellor

Von Schleicher controlled the new government from behind the scenes. He chose a wealthy gentleman politician, ex-General Franz von Papen, as the figurehead for this new coalition. Hindenburg made von Papen chancellor in May 1932.

Von Schleicher offered the NSDAP a place in the coalition. He thought he could control the Nazis, seeing them as 'merely children who had to be led by the hand'. Hitler agreed to the offer. From May 1932, therefore, Hitler and the Nazi Party were, for the first time, part of the government of Germany.

Source A: *this 1932 campaign poster for Hindenburg shows Germans at each other's throats. It said that Hindenburg was the only chance for peace.*

Activity

- Create a timeline for January 1932 to January 1933.
- Record on the timeline all the important political events of that time.
- Label the events to show the *causes* and the *significance* of each one.

40

Von Papen's coalition was weak from the start. In the general elections of July 1932, the NSDAP won 230 seats in the Reichstag. It was now the largest party. Hitler demanded that Hindenburg should sack von Papen and appoint him chancellor. Hindenburg, who had been field marshal of German forces during the First World War, detested Hitler – in his eyes he was a vulgar, jumped-up corporal. He refused.

Instead, von Papen hung on to office and called a new election for November 1932. He was gambling that the Nazi support would fall. Nazi seats in the Reichstag did fall to 196, but they were still the largest party. Without Hitler's support, von Papen could no longer command a majority in the Reichstag, nor the confidence of Hindenburg. Von Papen resigned.

Von Schleicher becomes chancellor

Thirty-nine business tycoons like Krupp, Siemens, Thyssen and Bosch signed a letter asking Hindenburg to appoint Hitler as chancellor. They thought that, with their donations to his party, they could control him. But Hindenburg was still opposed. On 2 December, he appointed von Schleicher as chancellor.

Von Schleicher was confident that support for the Nazis was fading. He told a visiting Austrian minister that 'Herr Hitler is no longer a problem; his movement is a thing of the past'. But he consistently failed to get a majority in the Reichstag. He informed Hindenburg that von Papen and Hitler were conspiring against him – as in fact they were – and that he needed Hindenburg to suspend the constitution and declare von Schleicher head of a military dictatorship. Hindenburg refused, but news of von Schleicher's plan leaked out and he lost any remaining support in the Reichstag. His time was up.

Hitler becomes chancellor

Throughout all this, von Papen had continued to plot against von Schleicher with Hindenburg and right-wing parties in the Reichstag. He told them that, if they supported Hitler as chancellor, with von Papen as vice-chancellor, they could make all the decisions themselves and use Hitler as a figurehead. He said he had Hitler 'in his pocket'.

So, reluctantly, Hindenburg agreed that there was no alternative. 'It is my unpleasant duty then to appoint this fellow Hitler as Chancellor,' he grumbled. And on 30 January 1933, Adolf Hitler was legally and democratically appointed chancellor of Germany.

> The men of the German Right thought that the clever von Papen could outwit the hysterical ex-corporal, who lacked experience of high office. They became the gravediggers of the Republic.

Source B: from Europe Since Napoleon, David Thomson (1957).

Examination question

Explain how the political scene in Germany changed between 1928 and the beginning of 1933.   (8 marks)

Tip: This is a question about *change*. See page 35 for advice about this type of question.

41

ResultsPlus
Watchout!

Some students confuse the *chancellor* and the *president*.

The *chancellor* was:
- the head of the German *government* – rather like our prime minister.

The *president* was:
- the head of the German *state* – rather like our queen or king.

Source C: *this 1933 British cartoon shows Hindenburg and von Papen lifting Hitler to power, while cursing him under their breath.*

THE TEMPORARY TRIANGLE.

VON HINDENBURG AND VON PAPEN *(together)*—
"FOR HE'S A JOLLY GOOD FELLOW,
FOR HE'S A JOLLY GOOD FELLOW,
FOR HE'S A JOLLY GOOD FE-EL-LOW,
    (Aside: "Confound him!")
AND SO SAY BOTH OF US!"

42

In the Unit 2 exam, you will be required to answer questions on one country. You will have to answer six questions: Question 1 (a), (b), (c) and (d); either Question 2 (a) or Question 2 (b); and either Question 3 (a) or Question 3 (b).

You only have an hour and 15 minutes to answer these questions. The number of marks available for each question helps you judge how long to spend on each answer, but as a guide you might consider allocating your time as follows:

Question 1 (a) 6 minutes	Question 1 (b) 8 minutes	Question 1 (c) 12 minutes
Question 1 (d) 12 minutes	Question 2 12 minutes	Question 3 25 minutes

Remember to leave a few minutes at the end to check your spelling, punctuation and grammar in your answers to questions 2 and 3. Here we are going to look at Question 1 (c) and (d).

Results**Plus**
Build Better Answers

Question 1 (c)

Tip: Question 1 (c) will ask you to use your knowledge of the topic to explain effects or consequences. There are 8 marks for this question and you are required to go into things in a little more depth than you have done on Question 1 (a) and (b). A suitable question would be:

Explain the effects of the Wall St Crash on Germany. (8 marks)

Student answer

The Wall St Crash had a terrible effect on Germany. As a result of the Crash, America went into economic depression and was forced to call in the loans it had made to other countries. Under the Dawes and Young Plans, America had lent large amounts of money to Germany. Once this money was recalled, the German economy also went into depression. Wages were cut and employees laid off. Unemployment rose from 1.8 million in 1929 to 6 million by 1933.

Examiner comments

This answer is very good on the economic effects, but it fails to mention the political effects. As it has not explained more than one effect, it would be marked in Level 2.

Let's rewrite the answer, adding information about the political effects.

The Wall St Crash had a terrible effect on Germany. As a result of the Crash, America went into economic depression and was forced to call in the loans it had made to other countries. Under the Dawes and Young Plans, America had lent large amounts of money to Germany. Once this money was recalled, the German economy also went into depression. Wages were cut and employees laid off. Unemployment rose from 1.8 million in 1929 to 6 million by 1933.
This had two important political effects. Firstly, because people were desperate, they turned to the Communist Party. The Communists almost doubled their seats in the Reichstag from the 50 they had in 1928 as people saw them as offering a radical solution to Germany's problems. The most important effect, however, was an even larger growth in support for the Nazis. Hitler campaigned not only against the weak Weimar government, but also against the threat of communism. Many middle and upper class Germans saw the Nazis as the saviors of Germany and, by 1933, Hitler had become chancellor.

We now have a very good Level 3 answer with the effects explained. As there is also a link drawn (though not strongly) between the growth of the Communists and the rise of the Nazis, this would score full marks.

ResultsPlus
Build Better Answers

Question 1 (d)

Tip: Question 1 (d) will ask you to use your knowledge to explain why something happened. In other words, this is a question about causation. Let's look at an example.

Explain why the Weimar government found it difficult to govern Germany in the years 1919–23. (8 marks)

Student answer

The Weimar government had a number of problems. The Treaty of Versailles imposed reparations of £6600 million on Germany and the country found it difficult to pay. Also there were uprisings from both left and right groups. In 1918, the Spartacists held an uprising, then in 1920 there was the Kapp Putsch and in 1923 the Munich Putsch. If that wasn't bad enough, in 1923 the government couldn't afford to pay reparations and the French occupied the Ruhr. Industrial production collapsed and the value of the mark plummeted. This lead to hyperinflation. The price of a loaf of bread was 1 mark in 1919 but by November 1923 it had gone up to 200,000 billion marks!

Examiner comments

The candidate knows all the reasons and has explained them to show how the Weimar government had difficulties. The cost of a loaf of bread is fascinating. However, what the candidate does not do is explain why these problems brought about the stated outcome (i.e. made it difficult for good government to happen).

Let's rework the answer to put in some statements that pin the explanation to the outcome. To help you they are in bold.

The Weimar government found it difficult because there were a number of problems. The Treaty of Versailles imposed reparations of £6,600 million on Germany and the country found it difficult to pay. **So the government was faced with a shortage of money and a country with a sense of grievance. That made it more difficult to govern.** Also there were uprisings from both left and right groups. In 1919, the Spartacists held an uprising, then in 1920 there was the Kapp Putsch and in 1923 the Munich Putsch. **It seemed like the government did not have full control of the country or the full support of the people. So it was difficult to rule effectively.** If that wasn't bad enough, in 1923 the government couldn't afford to pay reparations and the French occupied the Ruhr. Industrial production collapsed and the value of the mark plummeted. This lead to hyperinflation. The price of a loaf of bread was 1 mark in 1919 but by 1923 it had gone up to 100,000 million marks! **With the economy in such a terrible state, people lost faith in the government. The middle and upper classes lost their savings and so the Weimar government had to operate in the face of huge unpopularity and with the economy in tatters. It was impossible to rule well in those conditions.**

Now we have three good reasons, all closely linked to why the government could not operate effectively. This is what is required for top marks.

Key Topic 3: The Nazi dictatorship 1933–39

From 30 January 1933, Hitler was chancellor of Germany but his power was limited.

- The Weimar constitution controlled what the chancellor could do.
- Hindenburg retained all the powers of the president.
- Hitler's cabinet of eleven had only two other NSDAP members – Wilhelm Frick and Hermann Goering.
- NSDAP members numbered only about one-third of the Reichstag.

Most people thought other politicians would restrain Hitler. The *New York Times* observed 'The composition of the Cabinet leaves Herr Hitler no scope for his dictatorial ambition.' But they were wrong; Hitler soon became a dictator in Germany.

In this Key Topic you will study:

- the removal of all opposition to the Nazis, 1933–34
- the Nazi police state
- Nazi censorship and propaganda.

You will see how, by 1939, Hitler was both president and chancellor of Germany; the NSDAP was the only political party allowed; any opposition was brutally put down by the Gestapo and the Nazi Party had taken control of all aspects of life, including newspapers, radio, the universities, the arts and sport.

The removal of opposition, 1933-34

Learning objectives

In this chapter you will learn about:

- the Reichstag fire and the election of March 1933
- the Enabling Act, the banning of political parties and trade unions
- the Night of the Long Knives
- the death of President Hindenburg.

The Reichstag fire

On the evening of 27 February 1933, the Reichstag building was destroyed by a massive fire. A young Dutchman, a communist supporter named Marinus van der Lubbe, was caught on the site with matches and firelighters. He confessed and was put on trial with four others, though he claimed that he had acted alone. The other four were found not guilty and released; van der Lubbe was found guilty and executed.

But van der Lubbe's execution was not enough for Hitler; he saw the Reichstag fire as an opportunity to attack the communists. He had made a Nazi, Hermann Goering, the new chief of police. Goering and Hitler claimed that the evidence showed that van der Lubbe was part of a communist **conspiracy** against the government.

Hitler used the Reichstag fire to make Hindenburg declare a **state of emergency**. As long as Hindenburg supported him, Hitler could now use decrees to govern Germany. Next he persuaded Hindenburg to call an election for 5 March 1933. He hoped for more Nazi seats in the Reichstag. There was nothing unconstitutional about any of this.

However, before the election took place:

- Hitler issued the Decree for the Protection of the People and the State. This gave him powers to suspend the civil rights of German citizens. He was able to imprison political opponents and ban communist newspapers
- since he now controlled Germany's police force, Hitler could ensure that they turned a blind eye to the activities of the SA
- Hitler also persuaded Krupp and other industrialists to finance the Nazi campaign – 3 million marks were donated in just one meeting.

It was a bloody election campaign; violent clashes led to 70 deaths.

Source A: *a 1933 cartoon. Joseph Goebbels, head of Nazi propaganda, is shown pulling a communist plotter out of a box. Some people thought that Hermann Goering, Nazi chief of police, made up the plot to suit the Nazis. Some historians have even suggested that Goering arranged the fire.*

That's sheer rubbish! It may be a good police report, but it's not the kind of message I have in mind! Why mention a single man? There were 10 or even 20 men! The whole thing was a signal for a communist uprising.

Source B: *Goering, speaking while editing the draft press report of the Reichstag fire. He crossed out '1 cwt of incendiary (fire-causing) material' and changed it to '1000 cwt' – even when told that no single arsonist could carry such a weight. (1 cwt, or hundredweight, is equivalent to about 50 kg.)*

Now we'll show them! The German people have been soft too long. Every communist official must be shot. All communist deputies must be hanged this very night. All friends of the communists must be locked up. And that goes for the Social Democrats as well.

Source C: *Hitler, on the evening of the Reichstag fire.*

The Nazis broke windows and came through the holes. They opened fire; Hans Saile was shot in the stomach. Secretaries were driven with cudgels and daggers and locked up for hours. The regular police blocked off the surrounding streets. The Nazis looted the building under their very eyes. Documents were heaped on to a pyre and set alight. The fire burned for three days and nights.

Source D: *a Social Democrat describing a Nazi raid on the SPD headquarters before the general election of March 1933.*

When results were announced, the Nazis had increased their Reichstag members to 288. Hitler used his emergency powers to ban the Communists from taking up their 81 seats. With the support of the other nationalist parties, this gave Hitler a two-thirds majority in the Reichstag. This was crucial. He now had enough votes to change the constitution of the republic.

The Enabling Act

The Enabling Act changed the constitution of the Weimar Republic. Hitler forced it through the Reichstag in late March 1933. The full name of the act was the Law for the Removal of the Distress of the People and Reich. It gave Hitler the right to make laws for four years without the consent of the Reichstag. It was renewed in 1937.

The new law was passed by 444 votes to 94. In this sense, it was legal – even though Reichstag members were intimidated during the vote. However, in effect, it marked the end of democratic rule and of the Weimar Republic.

> The Kroll Opera House, where the Reichstag met since its palace had been damaged by fire, was packed. There were nearly 300 Nazi deputies and 50 or so Nationalist. There was a marked absence of Communists. There were fewer Social Democrats than could have been present, because some were in hospital, the victims of electoral violence; some had fled the country – and who could blame them?
>
> Along the corridors, SS men, in their sinister black and silver uniforms, had been posted; their legs apart and arms crossed, their eyes fixed and cruel, looking like messengers of doom.
>
> Outside, a mob of SA chanted threatening slogans: 'Give us the Bill or else fire and murder'. Their clamour was clearly audible within the chamber.

Source E: *an observer, Sir John Wheeler-Bennet, recalling the debate on the Enabling Act.*

Trade unions

Trade unions were potential sources of opposition to Hitler. Hitler believed that, if communists amongst working men were able to control their trade unions, the unions could be used, in strikes for example, to undermine the government. Therefore, in May 1933, Hitler used his new powers to ban trade unions and make strikes illegal.

Activity

Start a list of the things the Nazis did between January and March 1933 to consolidate their power. You will continue to add to your list over the next few pages.

Source F: *Nazi SA marching into the Reichstag on 23 March 1933 to intimidate members during the Enabling Act debate.*

46

Political parties

In July 1933, Hitler followed the ban on trade unions by issuing a decree to make all political parties in Germany illegal, except for the NSDAP.

> Article I: The National Socialist German Workers' Party constitutes the only political party in Germany.
>
> Article II: Whoever undertakes to maintain the organisation of another political party or to form a new political party shall be punished with penal servitude of up to three years or imprisonment of between six months and three years.

Source G: *Law against the Establishment of Parties, 14 July 1933.*

Local government

The next step was for Hitler to strengthen the central government in Berlin – which he controlled – and to weaken local government in Germany.

Under the Weimar constitution, all regions (Länder) of Germany had their own parliament, which ran local government in the area. By 1934, Hitler had control of the Reichstag – but he could not control the 18 Länder parliaments.

So, in January 1934, he abolished the Länder parliaments and declared that governors, appointed by him, would run every region of Germany.

Source H: *a British cartoon from July 1933. President Hindenburg holds up Hitler's hand in triumph and Hermann Goering, the Nazi chief of police, removes a heavy swastika from within Hitler's glove. The people chant Hitler's name while German liberties slump, stunned and chained, in the corner.*

ResultsPlus
Top Tip

Exam question: Explain how the political situation in Germany changed during 1933.
(8 marks)

Read the advice on page 35 about *change* questions.

A good answer to the question above will not just *list* the changes that took place; it will show any *links* between the changes. For example:

One change in the political situation was the Enabling Act (give details). This change was linked to another change. In May 1933, strikes by trade unions were made illegal. Hitler could only make this change because another change – the Enabling Act – gave him powers to pass laws without consulting the Reichstag.

Remember to take care over your spelling, punctuation and grammar for this question.

Activities

1   Continue your list of things the Nazis did from January 1933 to January 1934 to consolidate their power. Then start to analyse your list.

Mark the things they did which were:

- legal
- illegal.

Mark the things they did which were:

- done alone
- done with the help of others.

2   Finally, imagine Hitler is in court. The charge is that:

'Between the months of January and July 1933, Adolf Hitler illegally seized power in Germany.'

Make yourself Hitler's defence lawyer. Write your speech to the jury, telling them Hitler was innocent.

(Do you really think Hitler was innocent?)

The Night of the Long Knives

By the start of 1934, Hitler had made Germany a **one-party state**. He now made sure that he was the unrivalled leader of that one party – the Nazi Party.

Hitler feared Ernst Röhm, the leader of the SA.

- Röhm had merged an army veterans group, the Stahlhelm, with the SA. This brought SA numbers to three million. With so many SA members loyal to him, Röhm was in an ideal position to challenge Hitler.
- Röhm also opposed Hitler's policies. He criticised Hitler's links with rich industrialists and army generals. He wanted more socialist policies, to tax the rich and help the working classes.

The German Army also worried about the power of Röhm. After the Treaty of Versailles the army had only 100,000 men; it was dwarfed by the SA. Röhm wanted the SA to replace the German Army.

Leaders of the SS, like Himmler and Heydrich, resented Röhm too. They wanted to reduce the power of the SA, so that they could increase their own power and the status of the SS.

In 1934, leaders of the SS and the army warned Hitler that Röhm was planning to seize power. So, on 30 June 1934, Hitler arranged for Röhm and several other senior officers of the SA to be arrested, imprisoned and shot. This is known as the Night of the Long Knives.

Adolf is a swine. His old friends are not good enough for him. Adolf is turning into a gentleman. He wants to sit on a hilltop and pretend he is God.

Source I: *Röhm, drunk in 1934, quoted by H. Rauschning, in his book* Hitler Speaks *(1940).*

With an SS escort, the Führer knocked gently on Röhm's door: 'A message from Munich', he said in a disguised voice. 'Come in' Röhm shouted, 'the door is open'. Hitler tore open the door, fell on Röhm as he lay in bed, grabbed him by the throat and screamed, 'You are under arrest, you pig!' Then he turned him over to the SS.

Source J: *extracts from the diary of Alfred Rosenberg, a leading Nazi politician, for 30 June 1934.*

Röhm was taken to Stadelheim Gaol, where, on 1 July, an SS brigade leader arrived. He left a loaded pistol, with one bullet, in Röhm's cell, thereby inviting Röhm to commit suicide. After 15 minutes, hearing no sound, he entered the cell with his deputy, where they both shot him. In addition to Röhm, six other SA leaders were shot, on Hitler's orders, at Stadelheim.

In the middle of all this, von Papen, still vice-chancellor, protested to Goering. He was told that the SS had things under control and he should return home for his own safety. SS squads were rounding up suspects; one group reached von Papen's office before he did, shot his press secretary and arrested his staff.

Source K: *a French magazine cover from August 1934. Hitler is shown, bathed in blood and dagger drawn, with dead SA storm troopers all around him. The caption says 'The Butcher of Berlin'.*

Von Papen's home was surrounded and his telephone cut off – so much for having 'Hitler in his pocket'.

Over a period of about four days, about 400 people, including 150 senior members of the SA, were shot without trial. These included:

- General von Schleicher – the ex-chancellor – who was gunned down along with his wife. Goering announced they had been shot resisting arrest
- Gregor Strasser, a Nazi member with socialist views similar to Röhm, who was locked in a **Gestapo** cell before gunmen sprayed bullets through a window. A lone gunman entered to finish him off.

Hitler was now clearly acting illegally by murdering his rivals for power. He claimed to be doing this in the interests of Germany. Some Germans objected to the violence, but few knew how terrible it had been. Most were grateful that the SA, hated for their brutality, had been restrained.

The SA continued after 1934 but it was limited to giving muscle to the Nazi party and no longer rivalled the army. It was also now firmly under Hitler's control.

> I ordered the leaders of the guilty to be shot. If anyone asks why I did not use the courts of justice, I say this: in this hour, I was responsible for the fate of the German people and I became the supreme judge of the German people.

Source M: *Hitler, in a speech to the Reichstag on 13 July 1934.*

The death of President Hindenburg

Finally, on 2 August 1934, President Hindenburg died, aged 87, and Hitler moved in to take over supreme power.

- He declared himself Germany's Führer.
- He decreed that, as Führer, he would add all of the president's powers to those he already held as chancellor.
- He forced an oath of loyalty to him from every soldier in the army.

A **plebiscite** (public vote) was organised to confirm Hitler as the Führer. Bombarded by pro-Nazi propaganda, 90 per cent of voters decided in favour. The Weimar Republic had ended; Hitler's Third Reich had begun.

Source L: *a British cartoon from July 1934. The ranks of the SA are shown desperately saluting with both hands, as Hitler looks on with his gun still smoking.*

Examination question

Was the Reichstag fire the main reason why Hitler was able to establish a dictatorship in Germany by 1934? Explain your answer.

You may use the following information to help you:

- **the general election results of 1933**
- **the Enabling Act**
- **the banning of political parties and trade unions**
- **the Night of the Long Knives. (16 marks)**

Tip: There is advice about this type of question on page 39.

ResultsPlus
Watch out!

Weak answers to this type of question just describe causes. But the question doesn't ask 'What were the causes?' – it asks 'Was this the main cause?' Form an opinion and explain why you think this was or was not the main cause. You are being asked to construct an argument.

The Nazi police state

> ### Learning objectives
>
> In this chapter you will learn about:
> - Himmler, the SS and the Gestapo
> - Nazi concentration camps and the law courts
> - repression of the Church in Nazi Germany.

Nazi Germany was a police state. This is a state in which the government uses the police – sometimes secret police – to control people's lives. Views opposed to the Nazis were suppressed. The main organisations used by Hitler to exert this control over Germany were the SS and the Gestapo.

The SS (Schutzstaffel)

The SS was a military group, set up in 1925 as a personal bodyguard for Hitler. From 1929 it was run by Heinrich Himmler. The main role of the SS was to be the Nazi Party's own private police force. They were totally loyal to Hitler. It was the SS who warned him about Röhm in 1934 and Hitler used SS officers to murder SA leaders during the Night of the Long Knives. Gradually, during the 1930s, the SS was expanded to 50,000 men and put in charge of all the other state security services.

Another role of the SS was to carry out the Nazi policy of racial purification (see pages 68–71). One part of the SS was the Totenkopf (Death's Head Units), who ran concentration camps.

Himmler was careful about recruitment to the SS. He ensured that members were Aryan in appearance; they were expected to marry 'racially pure' wives.

The Gestapo

The Gestapo (Geheime Staatspolizei) was Hitler's non-uniformed secret police force. They were set up in 1933 by Hermann Goering and placed under the control of the SS in 1936. The Gestapo was led by Reinhard Heydrich. Germans particularly feared the Gestapo because they could not tell them apart from other members of the public. The Gestapo arrested people who acted against or spoke out in any way against Nazi ideas. Offenders could be imprisoned without trial.

All states have police forces. But in most states the police have to act within the law and can be held to account in the courts. However, the SS and Gestapo could arrest people without being responsible to anyone but their commanders and Hitler.

> Right from the start, I have taken the view that it does not matter in the least if our actions are against some clause in the law; in my work for the Führer and the nation, I do what my conscience and common sense tells me is right.

Source A: *Himmler addressing the Committee for Police Law in 1936.*

Source B: *Nazi SA. Their banner reads 'We don't like sabotage of the work of the Führer'. Their poster shows what the Nazis would not accept – whispered criticisms and a Jew being baptised as a Christian.*

> To discover the enemies of the state, watch them and render them harmless at the right moment…In order to fulfil this duty, the political police must be free to use every means suited to achieve the desired end.

Source C: *Werner Best, Heydrich's deputy.*

By 1939, 150,000 people were 'under protective arrest' in prisons. This means that they had not committed criminal acts, like stealing. They were just locked up for doing things that the Nazis disapproved of, such as voicing views opposed to Hitler and the Nazis. Once in the prisons, they were at the mercy of their guards.

Concentration camps

The first Nazi concentration camp was opened at Dachau in 1933. Later that year, the first camp for women was opened at Moringen. Camps were normally located in isolated areas outside cities and away from the public gaze. They were secretive places, not controlled by normal prison rules.

Inmates were mainly political prisoners or 'undesirables' – like prostitutes and minority groups, such as Jews – of whom the Nazis disapproved. From 1938 onwards, the SS used camp inmates as forced labour for business enterprises, for example producing army uniforms.

There were six concentration camps by 1939, holding about 20,000 people in total. After 1939, concentration camps grew in number and size and they were used for the mass murder of minority groups, such as the Jews.

The law courts

Finally, Hitler also took control of what happened in the courts. First, he set up the National Socialist League for the Maintenance of the Law. He insisted that all judges must be members. If any judges displeased the Nazis, they were denied membership.

Certain that judges would support Nazi ideas, Hitler gave them freedom to punish people even when they had not broken the law.

He also set up a new People's Court, to hear all treason cases – offences against the state. Judges for this court were hand picked. Even then, if Hitler thought sentences too lenient, he increased them himself.

In the SS, today, we have about one case of homosexuality a month. In each case, these people will be publicly degraded, expelled, and handed over to the courts. Following punishment imposed by the court, they will be sent, by my order, to a concentration camp, and shot in the concentration camp, while attempting to escape. Thereby, the increasingly healthy blood which we are cultivating for Germany, will be kept pure.

Source D: *Himmler, speaking to SS commanders, 18 February 1937.*

Physical punishment consisted of whipping, frequent kicking (in the abdomen or groin), slaps in the face, shooting or wounding with the bayonet. Prisoners were forced to stare for hours into glaring lights, to kneel for hours and so on.

Source E: *from* Concentration Camp Dachau: 1933-1945, *Barbara Distel and Ruth Jakusch, eds. (1978).*

The judge is to…arbitrate (pass judgement) in disagreements. The National Socialist ideology, as expressed in the party programme and the speeches of the Führer, is the basis for interpreting the law.

Source F: *Professor Karl Eckhardt, a Nazi legal expert, in 1936.*

The Führer has seen the press cutting about the sentencing of the Jew, Markus Luftgas, to two-and-a-half years in prison. He desires that Lufgas should be executed. Please make the arrangements.

Source G: *a letter from Hitler's private office, quoted in* World Conflict in the Twentieth Century, *by S.M. Harrison (1987).*

Activity

You are a prisoner in a German concentration camp in the 1930s.

- Write a letter to smuggle out of the camp. In the letter describe your arrest, treatment and experiences.
- The letter should be based on fact, not imagination. Use the information on these pages to provide detail for your letter.

Repression of the Church

The Christian religion was one aspect of Germany repressed by Hitler's police state. The likelihood of friction was obvious. Whereas the Nazis glorified strength and violence and taught racial superiority, Christianity preached tolerance and peace and respect for all people.

At first, Hitler tried to control the Christian churches by reassuring them and encouraging them to work with the Nazi government.

> Christianity is the unshakeable foundation of the moral and ethical life of our people. The National Government's concern will be for co-operation of the Church with the State. It expects, however, that [*this*] will meet with similar appreciation from their side.

Source H: *extract from a speech by Hitler in the Reichstag on the Enabling Law (March 1933).*

However, this approach didn't work for long. Soon, Hitler turned the full force of the police state against Christians.

The Catholic church

One-third of Germany's Christians were Catholic. Again, there were obvious sources of friction here.

- On social issues, Catholics owed their first allegiance, not to Hitler, but to the Pope.
- Catholics also had their own schools, which taught values different from Nazi state schools.

Hitler tried, at first, to reach agreement with the Catholic Church. In July 1933, he reached a concordat (agreement) with the Pope. Hitler agreed:

- to confirm freedom of worship for Catholics
- not to interfere with Catholic schools in Germany.

The Roman Catholic Church:

- agreed that its priests would not interfere in politics
- ordered German bishops to swear loyalty to the National Socialist regime.

> In my spiritual office, for the welfare and interest of the German Reich, I will endeavour to avoid all detrimental acts which might endanger it.

Source J: *extract from the oath of allegiance to the Nazi regime, sworn by German Catholic bishops in 1933.*

Source I: *this NSDAP poster from 1933 shows the swastika knocking out the Catholics and the communists. This suggests that Hitler was always half-hearted about working with the Catholic Church.*

Source K: *a French cartoon from 1933. The Pope is shown, on the right, encouraging a priest to accept Hitler. Notice that the hands holding Hitler's photo also hold a club.*

But Hitler didn't keep his promise to the Catholic Church. As the 1930s went on:

- Catholic priests were harassed and arrested; many ended up in concentration camps
- Catholic schools were brought in line with state schools or closed
- Catholic youth activities, like the Catholic Youth League, were banned.

By 1937, Pope Pius XI realised that the Concordat was worthless. He issued a stinging criticism of the Nazi regime in a statement known as 'Mit Brennender Sorge' ('With Burning Anxiety').

The Protestant church

Hitler also fell out with Christians in the Protestant churches. At first, some Protestants were so grateful that Hitler had protected them from anti-Christian communists that they worked with the Nazis. They even allowed Nazi flags to be displayed inside their churches. These Protestants formed the German Christian Movement. Its leader was Ludwig Müller. Hitler made Müller the Reich bishop of Germany in September 1933. Protestant pastors who supported Hitler were allowed to carry on with their church services as normal.

However, many Protestant Christians opposed Hitler's policies; some even spoke out against him. The most famous of these was Pastor Martin Niemöller. In 1933, he was one of the Protestant pastors who set up the Pastors' Emergency League (PEL), to campaign against Nazi actions. These Protestants became increasingly troublesome to Hitler. In 1937, Niemöller was sent to a concentration camp along with hundreds of his fellow ministers.

By this time, Hitler controlled the Reichstag, the NSDAP, the army, the police and the legal system. He treated the Christian Church with contempt. This was truly a **totalitarian state**, in which the central government controlled every aspect of the country.

Source M: in this British cartoon from 1934, the onlookers are saying, 'It is rumoured that Führer-President-Chancellor Hitler, unable to settle Germany's religious mutiny in any other way, contemplates taking over yet another high office'.

Examination question

Describe the key features of the police state in Nazi Germany. **(6 marks)**

Tip: This is a question about *key features*. Advice about this type of question is given on page 21.

We all know that, if the Third Reich were to collapse, communism would come in its place. Therefore, we must show loyalty to the Führer, who has saved us from communism and given us a better chance.

Source L: *a leader of the German Christian Church, 1937.*

Did you know?

Martin Neimöller was a hero of the First World War, a submarine captain and Nazi sympathiser. He set up the Protestant Confessional Church and openly attacked Nazi anti-semitism.

Censorship and propaganda

Learning objectives

In this chapter you will learn:
- how the Nazis used censorship to ban information and ideas which they didn't like
- how the Nazis used propaganda to publicise information and ideas which they wanted to promote.

Nazi Germany was a totalitarian state. This means a state in which the government seeks to control all individuals and every aspect of society. Censorship and propaganda were two of the ways the Nazis exerted this control. Sometimes, censorship and propaganda were linked. For example, the Nazis stopped the press printing some news (censorship) and told them what to print instead (propaganda).

As you saw on pages 34–35, from 1929, Joseph Goebbels had been in charge of Nazi propaganda. When Hitler became chancellor in 1933, Goebbels was made the Minister of People's Enlightenment and Propaganda. So he controlled Nazi censorship and propaganda, which were not used just to control people's political views and actions, but also their artistic and cultural views.

The press

Newspapers were encouraged by the Nazis – but they had to provide views which the Ministry agreed with or face the consequences. Journalists were given regular briefings, containing the information the government were willing to publicise; they were sometimes given direct instructions what to write.

Under these circumstances, there could be no free press in Germany; every newspaper was a Nazi newspaper.

ResultsPlus
Watch out!

Some students confuse *Goebbels* with *Goering*.
Remember, it was:
- Goering who was Hitler's chief of police
- Goebbels who was Hitler's minister for censorship and propaganda.

In the next issue, there must be a lead article, featured as prominently as possible, in which the decision of the Führer, no matter what it may be, will be discussed as the only possible one for Germany.

Source A: *Ministry of Public Enlightenment and Propaganda instruction to press, September 1939.*

Photos showing members of the Reich government at dining tables in front of rows of bottles must not be published in future. This has given the absurd impression that members of the government are living it up.

Source B: *Ministry of Propaganda order, 1935.*

Source C: *this 1935 British cartoon shows Hitler and Goering entertaining British visitors to Germany. Goebbels takes a cosy press photo. But there is violence hidden behind the scenes.*

Universities

The Nazis had little respect for academic research. The Nazi Education Minister once said 'A road-sweeper sweeps 1000 microbes with a stroke; a scientist preens himself on discovering a single microbe'. Between 1933 and 1938, 3000 professors or lecturers were dismissed from jobs.

Research was heavily directed by the Ministry and the results were expected to support Nazi views. All academics who remained had to agree publicly to things which were clearly nonsense (see below).

> Physics is the creation of the German mind…In fact, all European science is the fruit of Aryan thought.

Source D: *the Director of the Institute of Physics, in Dresden.*

The arts

Goebbels also controlled the arts. He set up the Reich Chamber of Culture. Writers, musicians, artists and actors had to be members. Those of whom the Nazis disapproved were banned.

The Nazis decided what literature would be available to the German people. Books with views which they didn't like were censored. Millions of books were taken from university and public libraries and burned on huge, public bonfires. On one occasion, students in Berlin burned 20,000 books written by Jews, communists and anti-Nazi authors, destroying books, for example, by Freud, Einstein and Thomas Mann.

Music was also censored. Jazz music was banned; it was seen as black music and therefore inferior. The work of Mendelssohn was also banned because he was partly Jewish. Richard Wagner, in contrast, was promoted because he put to music heroic German legends from the past. Beethoven, Bach and traditional German folk music were also favoured.

As an artist, Hitler had very strong views in this area and art was heavily censored on racial or political grounds, or just as a matter of taste. The Ministry disapproved, for example, of almost all modern art. The Nazis preferred art which showed images of perfect German men and women or heroic German folk tales.

In the theatre, plays about German history and politics were favoured as long as they reflected Nazi views. For this reason, cheap theatre tickets were made available – plays were a good way of getting Nazi views across.

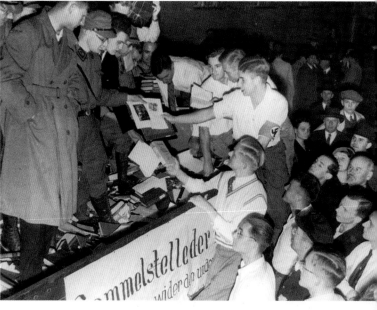

Source E: *burning books. In 1933, a Nazi student group declared 10 May to be a national day for burning 'un-German books', which were destroyed in towns all across Germany.*

Activities

1   Make a table to show Nazi censorship and propaganda.

● Make 'Censorship' and 'Propaganda' your two columns.

● Make the press, universities, books, etc., your rows.

2   As you read this chapter, when you find examples of censorship or propaganda, describe them in your table.

   Remember, in some areas, the Nazis used both censorship and propaganda.

3   Continue your table for the next two pages.

By the 1930s, Goebbels had learned many ways to publicise the Nazi Party. But from 1933, Goebbels could use all the resources of the government to publicise Hitler and his views on every aspect of society. Some of these ways just continued methods used by the Nazis in the 1920s. For example:

- government posters were used to advertise Nazi views
- Goebbels expanded his use of rallies and parades. A mass rally was held each year at Nuremberg to create a sense of German unity and advertise the strength of the Nazi Party
- aeroplanes were used to transport Hitler quickly from place to place, so that he could be seen in person by millions of Germans.

Some methods were new, such as radio and cinema.

Radio

Goebbels started to use the power of the radio.

- All radio stations were put under Nazi control.
- Hitler and other Nazi officials made frequent broadcasts.
- Cheap mass-produced radios were sold or placed in cafes, factories and schools; speakers were even placed in the street. By the 1930s there were more radios per person in Germany than anywhere in Europe.

Cinema

Goebbels also influenced films shown at cinemas. With audiences of over 250 million in 1933, they obviously had excellent potential for getting Nazi views across.

- Films were shown alongside a 45-minute official newsreel, publicising Germany's achievements.
- From 1934, film-makers had to send the plot of every new film to Goebbels for approval.
- Some films had overtly political messages, like *Hitlerjunge Quex* (1933), in which a young member of the Nazi party was killed by communists.

Did you know?

Hitler and Goebbels noticed the popularity of Mickey Mouse films so they had a propaganda cartoon made. The leading character, Hansi, was a canary, with three fingers in white gloves, just like Mickey, but with Hitler's lick of hair across his forehead. In the film, Hansi was pestered by villainous black crows with Jewish features.

Crowning the stadium was a giant eagle with a 100-foot wing-spread, thousands of swastika banners and 130 anti-aircraft searchlights with a range of 25,000 feet.

When 200,000 Party faithful, with 20,000 flags crowded in, the effects of gleaming searchlight pillars was breathtaking. Hitler's voice came across the field with eerie effect.

Source F: *extracts from* Adolf Hitler *by John Toland, 1976, describing the 1934 Nuremburg Rally.*

Attention! On Wednesday 21st March, the Führer is speaking on all German (radio) stations from 11am to 11.50 am…All factory owners, stores, offices, shops, pubs and flats must put up speakers an hour before, so that the whole workforce can hear.

Source G: *Ministry of Propaganda order, March 1934.*

GOEBBELS, RINGMASTER OF THE REICH'S CULTURE CIRCUS

Source H: *Joseph Goebbels was very different from Hitler. He was younger and an intellectual – he had a PhD in literature and philosophy. But, like Hitler, he was a powerful speaker. This American cartoon, from 1938, shows him as the Ringmaster of the Nazi Circus.*

Sport

Hitler and Goebbels also used sport to show Nazi Germany in a good light. Their best opportunity to do this came in 1936, when the Olympic Games were held in Berlin.

Source I: the Olympic flame enters the Olympic stadium in Berlin. Note that the flags in the background are not the German flag, but the Nazi flag.

> ### Did you know?
> Gretel Bergmann was the women's high-jump champion for Germany. She was in the Olympic team, but she was Jewish. The Germans also picked another German high jumper, Dora Ratjen, who beat Gretel. Later, Dora Ratjen was found to be a man – a member of the Hitler Youth, picked to ensure that a Jewish German woman could not win a gold medal.

- The Nazis built an Olympic stadium which could hold 110,000 people and was the largest in the world, to reflect the power of Germany.
- All the events were faultlessly organised, to show off German efficiency.
- Germany won 33 gold medals, more than any other country – and more silver and bronze too. The Nazis claimed this was proof of Aryan superiority.

There was only one embarrassment for the Nazis; the black American athlete, Jesse Owens, broke Olympic records 11 times in heats and finals and won four gold medals. Hitler refused to present medals to any of the nine black US medal winners.

Hitler the figurehead

A key feature of Nazi propaganda was Hitler himself. National Socialism depended upon loyalty to one national leader, who would be trusted to act in the best interests of the whole nation. So Hitler's image was carefully crafted. He was the one who united the nation. He was shown as strong and decisive. But he was also frequently pictured with children to show that he was a caring father figure.

> The crowd looked up to Hitler with touching faith, as their helper, their saviour, their deliverer from distress…He is the rescuer of the scholar, the farmer, the worker and the unemployed.

Source K: an extract from the diary of Luise Solmitz, writing in 1932. She was a schoolteacher who heard Hitler speak at a meeting in Hamburg.

Ein Volk, ein Reich, ein Führer!

Source J: a portrait of Hitler, showing him as a strong, statesman-like leader. The caption is 'One People, One Reich, One Führer'.

58

In the Unit 2 exam, you will be required to answer questions on one country. You will have to answer six questions: Question 1 (a), (b), (c) and (d); either Question 2 (a) or Question 2 (b); and either Question 3 (a) or Question 3 (b). You have only one hour and 15 minutes to answer these questions.

Here we are going to look at Question 2 (a) and (b).

Build Better Answers

Question 2 (a)

Tip: Question 2 (a) and (b) will ask you to use your knowledge to explain how something changed or developed. Remember that for this question there are up to 3 additional marks available for spelling, punctuation and grammar.

(a) Explain how Hitler established his authority in Germany in the years 1933 and 1934. (8 marks)

Student answer	Examiner comments
In 1933 Hitler became chanseller. To make sure of no opposition he past the enabling act this ment that he had the power to draw up laws without having to go to parlament.	It is true that the Enabling Act was an important part of Hitler's power base, but the candidate has not said why it was important, or how else Hitler established his authority. It's also not quite true that 'Hitler passed the Enabling Act'. The Reichstag did. This would be a weak Level 2 answer. The spelling, punctuation and grammar are also poor.

Let's rewrite the answer with that additional detail.

In 1933 Hitler became chancellor. To make sure that there was no opposition to him, he arranged for the Reichstag to pass the Enabling Act. This meant that he had the power to draw up laws and make changes to the constitution without having to go to the Reichstag. It was a very important measure in establishing his authority because now he did not need to worry about persuading the Reichstag to pass his laws, he could do what he wanted. Hitler had persuaded the Reichstag to pass the law by stationing troops around the parliament building. That was typical of the force he used in those years. We can see this in another way he established his authority. The SA had been like his private army in the years leading up to him becoming chancellor. Now they were too powerful and stopped Hitler getting the support of the regular army. So on the Night of the Long Knives he arrested and executed the SA leaders. That's how he got authority – by force. Now the army leaders were happy to support him, and some rivals for leadership of the party were dead.	There is a lot more that could be said here, but the candidate has explained two ways in which Hitler established his authority (the Enabling Act and the Night of the Long Knives) and how those measures increased his authority. It is a good Level 3 answer. The spelling, punctuation and grammar are also much improved in this answer.

ResultsPlus
Build Better Answers

Question 2 (b)
Let us now look at Question 2 (b). This time, instead of looking at a student answer and examiner's comment, we will trace the thought processes of the student as they write their answer.

A suitable question would be:

(b) Explain how Hitler dealt with the problem of unemployment in Germany in the years 1933–39. (8 marks)

Student's thought process	Student's answer
Why the dates 1933-39? That's from when Hitler became chancellor to the outbreak of the war. What about unemployment? I know about how Hitler reduced it, but I'd probably better just state the problem. I don't suppose the marks are for that, though, so I'll keep it short.	When Hitler came to power in 1933 Germany was suffering from economic problems and unemployment had risen to 6 million. The Weimar government had failed to deal with it and Hitler knew he had to if he was to stay in power.
Now I need to say what basic ways I think it was done and add some details to prove it. They are: creating jobs, controlling the work force, using the army.	One of the ways that Hitler dealt with the problem of unemployment was by providing jobs on government projects. People found jobs working on public works schemes building motorways, hospitals and schools, for example. This not only stopped them being unemployed but also helped stimulate the economy by providing wages to buy goods.

Another way was by controlling the workforce. Millions of workers were organised into the National Labour Service and told where they could work. Trade unions were banned and a Nazi organisation called the German Labour Front was set up. This was more about controlling 'difficult' workers but it was also part of increasing the numbers in work – though on lower wages.

A third way of reducing unemployment was to increase the numbers in the armed forces. Military spending rose from less than 5 billion marks a year in 1933 to 25 billion in 1938. Obviously a lot of that went on weapons, but there were 750,000 more soldiers in 1938 than in 1933, so that brought unemployment down. |
| Anything else I can add? Perhaps something about women? I'll add a short summary. | It is also true that women were encouraged to stay at home and have babies. So that must have reduced unemployment too by creating jobs for men where there had been women workers e.g. as doctors and teachers.

What all these things have in common is that they were measures based on control. The Nazi state told people what to do. Work here, don't join the union, join the army, etc. But they did bring unemployment down to only 218,000 by 1938. |

Key Topic 4: Nazi domestic policies 1933-39

Hitler and the NSDAP had come to power largely by attacking the actions and policies of others. Germans supported the National Socialists because they feared communism, because they despaired at the failure of the moderate parties and because Hitler promised a new, strong and unified Germany. Once he came to power, in 1933, Hitler had to turn that promise into actual policies. This section describes what it was like to live in Germany, governed by Hitler and the National Socialist Party.

In this Key Topic you will study:

- Nazi policies towards women and the young
- employment and the standard of living
- the persecution of minorities.

Youth and education in Nazi Germany

> ## Learning objectives
>
> In this chapter you will learn about:
> - schools in Nazi Germany
> - Hitler's youth movements
> - opposition to Hitler among some young people.

Nazis had very different ideas about boys and girls. Boys were directed towards paid work and the military. Girls were intended to be good wives and mothers. This shaped all Nazi policies towards German children.

Schools

All children attended school until they were 14 years old. After that, school was voluntary. Boys and girls went to separate schools.

New subjects were added to spread Nazi opinions, such as Race Studies, in which pupils were told that Aryans were superior and that they should not marry Jews. *Mein Kampf* became a compulsory school text. PE was allocated about one-sixth of school time, to keep young people healthy. Domestic science, including cookery and needlework, was compulsory for girls. Subjects like history and mathematics became vehicles for Nazi political views.

Youth movements

Outside school, the Nazi government ran a series of youth movements. Boys started, aged 6, in the Pimpf (Little Fellows) and did camping and hiking. When they reached 14, they could join the Hitler Jungvolk (Hitler Youth), which did military training, just like the SA. Girls were in separate groups, like the League of German Maidens. Girls focused on training for health and motherhood.

Nowhere in Hitler's own brand of socialism was class equality clearer than in the youth and labour movements, where young people of all classes came together without distinction.

The breezy posters and massed rallies give us the impression that all young Germans were keen on Hitler Youth. The truth is probably that many were, but many others attended half-heartedly and some because they were frightened not to. Some youngsters joined rival groups, who found simple ways to rebel. They grew their hair long or listened to modern swing music. Their groups were often mixed-sex groups. They sometimes daubed anti-Nazi slogans on walls. The most well known of these groups was the Edelweiss Pirates, which had about 2000 members by 1939.

Source A: *a German school in 1935. Teachers had to swear an oath of loyalty to Hitler and join the Nazi Teachers' League. They were expected to pass on Nazi political views. Teachers taught the Nazi salute and started each lesson with the children saying 'Heil Hitler'. Nazi posters and flags decorated classrooms.*

> The Jews are aliens in Germany. In 1933 there were 66,060,000 people in Germany of whom 499,862 were Jews. What is the percentage of aliens in Germany?

Source B: *question from a German maths textbook, 1933.*

Source C: *a 1935 poster for the League of German Maidens. Note the Aryan girl, her confidence and the Nazi flags.*

Women in Nazi Germany, 1933-39

Learning objectives

In this chapter you will learn about:
- Nazi views on the role of women
- Nazi policies to increase marriage and childbirth
- opposition to Nazi views on women.

During the 1920s, women's lives changed in most European countries. For example, in Weimar Germany:

- women over 20 years were given the vote and there were about 20 female members of the Reichstag
- women were also more likely to go out to work than in previous years and more likely to work in the professions, where they were often paid on an equal basis to men. For example, there were about 100,000 female teachers in Germany by 1933
- women also started to enjoy more social activities outside the family and express their freedom in the way they dressed.

But the Nazis had a very different view of how women should fit into society. They believed that, like Germany's youth, women should serve their society, and the best way that they could do this was to be good mothers.

To be good mothers, German women should:

- stay healthy
- learn housecraft – cookery and needlework
- marry and enable their husbands to be useful workers
- have children and bring them up to be good Germans
- stay at home and concentrate on domestic matters, not work or politics.

Furthermore, 'good' German women were not expected to wear make-up or trousers, or to dye or perm their hair.

When the Nazis came to power, their policies towards women were driven by these ideas.

- The German Women's Enterprise was formed, to arrange classes and radio broadcasts, teaching good motherhood.
- Women were encouraged to leave work and concentrate on the 3Ks – *kinder, küche, kirche* (children, kitchen and church).
- Some professional women were forced to leave their jobs as doctors, lawyers or teachers.

Nazi policies towards women had the extra benefit for the Nazis of freeing up jobs for men – and thus reducing unemployment.

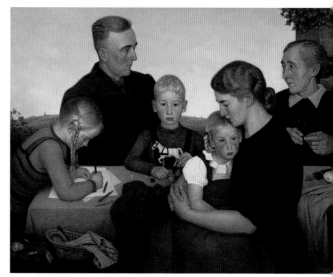

Source A: *a 1939 painting called 'A Farming Family from Kalinberg'. The painting reflects Nazi ideas of the dominant male figure and women concerned with children and housework.*

Source B: *girls in the League of German Maidens practising their housecraft in preparation for motherhood. Nazi policies towards girls were driven by their views on women.*

Marriage and childbirth

The **birth rate** was falling in Nazi Germany, and the Nazis wanted to reverse this. So, as well as their general views on the role of women listed above, they had several policies specifically intended to increase marriage and childbirth.

- In 1933, the Law for the Encouragement of Marriage was introduced. Loans of 1000 marks, worth about nine months' wages, were provided for young couples to marry, as long as the wife left work. For each one of their first four children, the couple could keep a quarter of the loan. There were other payments to encourage childbirth too.

- The Mother's Cross also encouraged childbirth. It was an award given to women for the number of children they had: bronze for four or five children, silver for six or seven children, and gold for eight or more children. Each year from 1939, on 12 April (Hitler's mother's birthday), medals were distributed to women with large families.

I was proud. When I got the gold, there was a big celebration in a school, where the mothers were all invited for coffee and cake.

Source D: *Wilhelmine Haferkamp, who eventually had ten children.*

- The Lebensborn (meaning 'fountain of life') programme was another policy to encourage childbirth. This was started in 1935 by the SS leader, Heinrich Himmler. At first, the policy just provided nurseries and financial aid for women who had children with SS men. Later, it even made 'single women available for fertilisation by SS men'. This was to create 'genetically pure' children for adoption by worthy German families. In one home alone, over 540 mothers gave birth from 1938 to 1941.

By the end of the 1930s, German industry was expanding so fast that the Nazis needed women to do some work, so some of their earlier policies were reversed. Nevertheless, fewer women were working in Germany in the late 1930s than had been working during the early 1920s.

Hitler believed that these policies were fair to women. In a speech in 1935, he said: 'Both sexes have their rights, their tasks. These tasks are equal in dignity and value.' But some women remained strongly opposed to this view of women. Some even said that the Nazi view of women encouraged men to see women as inferior.

A son, even the youngest, laughs in his mother's face. He regards her as his servant and women in general are merely willing tools of his aims.

Source F: *extract from a letter to a Leipzig newspaper in 1934.*

I got 30 marks per child from the Hitler government and 20 marks from the city. That was a lot of money. I sometimes got more 'child money' than my husband earned.

Source C: *Wilhelmine Haferkamp, who was 22 years old in 1933.*

Source E: *other political parties were very aware that Nazi policies towards women were unpopular with many women. This Social Democrat poster shows a downtrodden woman strapping up the boots of a harsh, unfeeling Nazi.*

Examination question

Explain how the position of women changed in the years 1933–39.   (8 marks)

Tip: This is a question about *change*. There has been advice given about change questions in earlier chapters. Look up that advice (on page 35) to help you with your answer.

Work and employment, 1933-39

> **Learning objectives**
>
> In this chapter you will learn about:
> - Hitler's policies for German workers
> - Hitler's policies for Germany's unemployed
> - Hitler's policy of rearmament and its economic effects.

The Nazis intended to make the economy, just like youth and women, serve the needs of the state.

Nazi policy towards workers

Hitler believed that powerful trade unions could disrupt the economy, so the government banned these in 1933. In their place, Hitler set up the DAF (German Labour Front). The DAF's key role was to ensure that workers served the best interests of the Nazi regime.

However, to ensure that the economy worked for the best interests of the state, the DAF also controlled the power of the employers. It set out new employment rights of all workers in factories, mines, munitions plants and shipyards. It regulated working hours (which increased on average by six hours per week) and rates of pay. The DAF also had powers to punish workers.

Although German workers lost their freedom to act collectively against employers, at least the DAF established what the minimum working standards should be, which prevented serious exploitation of labour by employers.

(It was) a system in which owners of property and workers were all subjects of the state. The great industrial magnates, like Krupp and Thyssen, remained – but they were forced to serve the needs of Germany. Trade unions were abolished… labour was put at the disposal of the Reich, in the form of the new Labour Front.

Source A: *from* Europe Since Napoleon, *David Thomson (1957).*

Nazi policy towards the unemployed

Solving unemployment was important to Hitler for many reasons. Unemployed workers were potential supporters of the communists, Hitler's rivals. Nazis also believed that unemployed workers sapped the strength of a nation. Men needed to be put to useful work, in the service of their country.

So, in 1933 the Nazis set up the RAD (National Labour Service). This provided manual work for the unemployed. At first it was a voluntary scheme, but from 1935 it was made compulsory for all young men to serve for six months in the RAD.

Men in the RAD were organised along the lines of an army. Workers wore uniforms, lived in camps and did military drill and parades as well as work. Rates of pay were very low and some complained of very poor food. Those in the RAD were used to work in the fields and build public buildings and autobahns (motorways). Apart from giving men work, these projects were also good for Germany. By 1939, Germany had 7000 miles of autobahns.

Source B: *Hitler starts the first autobahn project, 1933.*

Rearmament

As you have seen, the Nazi view was that the health of a nation depended upon constant struggle against other nations and that the German race needed Lebensraum (living space outside its existing borders). These views required military power. Therefore, Nazi policy towards the economy – like its policy towards youth – was organised to make Germany strong as a military nation.

In 1936, Hitler issued a secret memo declaring that the economy must be reorganised to make Germany able to wage war within four years. Hitler's 'Four Year Plan' had several effects on the economy.

- Government spending on **rearmament** increased:
  - in 1933, spending on arms was 3.5 billion marks
  - by 1939, it was 26 billion marks.
- The army's need for iron and steel increased:
  - German production of these trebled from 1933 to 1939.
- The government wanted to reduce the damage any naval blockade might do so they boosted German production of products like plastic, oil and rubber: in order to be self-sufficient (**autarky**)
  - German production of plastic increased by 460% in the 1930s.
- The German army grew; it numbered:
  - about 100,000 in 1933
  - about 500,000 in 1936
  - about 900,000 in 1939.

As the army increased in size so demand for uniforms and equipment also grew. In economic terms, rearmament was a huge boost for Germany. Unemployment went down, while production and profits went up.

> In the Third Reich, the main function of the economy was to provide resources to fight wars.
>
> **Source C:** *from* Nazism and War, *Richard Bessel (2004).*

Overall

There were political benefits for some of Hitler's actions. Banning unions and reducing unemployment reduced political opposition to the Nazis. There were social benefits too. Protecting workers' rights and reducing unemployment helped all ordinary Germans – workers and their families. Unemployment fell from 4.8 million in 1933 to 1.6 million in 1936 and 0.5 million in 1938. There were also military reasons for Hitler's actions: by 1939, Germany was ready for war.

However, funding public works and rearmament was expensive. In addition, some of the employment had only been achieved by moving women and Jews out of jobs and by expanding organisations like the SS and Gestapo.

Source D: *this 1938 British cartoon shows Hitler using his political power to make the army and the economy work together for the benefit of the state.*

ALL QUIET ON THE NAZI FRONT.

The standard of living, 1933-39

> **Learning objectives**
>
> In this chapter you will learn about:
> - rises in employment, wage levels and consumer spending
> - changes in working conditions
> - rises in prices
> - the overall effect of all these on German living standards.

The Nazi economy was organised to strengthen the state. But Hitler tried to balance this by improving **living standards** for workers. He knew that his political survival could depend upon this. Historians have argued whether, overall, the standard of living did improve.

The case for a rising standard of living

As you saw in the previous chapter, unemployment had drastically reduced in Germany by 1939. More people in work meant more people enjoying the benefits of a regular income.

Wage levels also improved and one sign of people's higher spending power was that sales of consumer goods (for example, clothes and household goods) also increased.

Years	Percentage rise in wages compared to 1933 levels
1934	6 per cent
1936	13 per cent
1938	20 per cent

Years	Percentage increase in sales compared to 1933 levels
1934	14 per cent
1936	25 per cent
1938	45 per cent

For some people, luxury purchases increased too. The Nazis supported the production of a new people's car (Volkswagen), which was meant to make car ownership possible for the masses.

Hitler asked Ferdinand Porsche to design a vehicle for four people which would do 40 miles to the gallon and which the average German could afford. The number of car owners in Germany trebled in the 1930s.

Hitler also set up two organisations to help working conditions.

- One was the SdA – Beauty of Labour. This organisation tried to ensure good standards at work – of safety, cleanliness, lighting, noise levels, ventilation –and hot meals.
- The other was the KdF – Kraft durch Freude (Strength through Joy). This provided leisure activities for workers, including sports facilities, films, outings and theatre shows. The most loyal workers could win impressive holidays. KdF became the world's largest tour operator of the 1930s.

So we can see improvements in living standards. Hitler hoped people would recognise that they were better off than those in communist countries and that workers would see hard work as a noble thing – hence the SdA's name. It worked. Public support for Hitler after 1933 was mainly due to his economic success.

> Infant mortality has been reduced and is considerably lower than in Great Britain. Tuberculosis and other diseases have noticeably diminished. The criminal courts have never had so little to do. It is a pleasure to observe the physical aptitude of German youth. Even the poorest persons are better clothed than was formerly the case.

Source A: *Sir Arnold Wilson MP, a seven-time visitor to the Nazi regime.*

The case against a rising standard of living

Improvements in living standards were balanced by other changes.

- With trade unions banned, workers' freedoms had been reduced and their working hours had increased, on average from 43 hours a week to 49 hours.
- Many of the employed were in the military rather than productive jobs – or they were doing compulsory work for the Labour Service in very poor conditions.
- According to J. Bradford DeLong, an American historian, rising prices cancelled out wage increases. He says that food prices rose by 20 per cent in Germany between 1933 and 1939. This was because the Nazis limited farm output in order to keep farmers' incomes high.
- Finally, during the Great Depression of 1929–33, standards of living were very low; so any improvements measured against 1933 were really just a return to normal.

In addition, Germany could not have sustained Hitler's economic policies for long. Until 1936, German imports and exports were balanced. However, Hitler's policy of rearmament after 1936 meant that:

- the government was spending more than its income from taxes
- imports started to rise much higher than exports. Like individuals, countries can't go on spending more than they earn.

If war had not intervened in 1939, Germany would have started to run out of money, the economy would have stalled and living standards would have fallen again.

ResultsPlus
Build Better Answers

Exam question: Were improved wages the main effect of the Nazi economic policies?
(16 marks)

You may use the following information to help you with your answer:
- **rising wages**
- **falling unemployment**
- **working conditions**
- **price rises.**

Spelling, punctuation and grammar: 4 marks.

● **A good answer (level 2)** gives details about one or more effects of Nazi policy.

▲ **A better answer (level 3)** provides details about more than one effect and shows why one was more important than the others.

▲ **An excellent answer (level 4)** shows the connections between effects when explaining why one was most important.
For example: *It is true that one effect was that wages went up (give details). But, people didn't really gain from this because of rising prices (give details). They are linked. The rising prices meant that rising wages were not the most important effect.*

GUNS OR BUTTER ?

Did you know?

The Volkswagen project was not as noble as it appeared. The head of the DAF, Doctor Robert Ley, persuaded many people to start paying for cars on hire purchase before they went into production. None of these customers had received a car before war broke out in 1939. The Volkswagen plant was then converted to arms production. None of the money was refunded.

Source B: *as this 1936 British cartoon shows, after 1936, Hitler had a difficult choice about how to spend government money – on arms for Germany or food for the public.*

Persecution of minorities, 1933–39

Learning objectives

In this chapter you will learn about:

- the persecution of the Jews in Nazi Germany
- Nazi persecution of other racial minorities
- Nazi persecution of other minority groups in society.

Activity

There are many dates and events in this chapter. To help you to visualise these events, make a timeline from 1933 to 1939.

- Above the line, record events about the **persecution** of Jews.
- Below the line, record events about the persecution of other minority groups.

Anti-Semitism: the background

Anti-Jewish views, often referred to as anti-Semitism, had been common in Europe for centuries. There were several reasons:

- their religion, customs and looks made Jews stand out as 'different'
- some Christians hated Jews, blaming them for the execution of Christ.

When times were hard, people looked for scapegoats and sometimes blamed the Jews. For example, many Germans wrongly blamed the Jews for defeat in the First World War. Sometimes views about Jews were contradictory. For example, Jews were criticised for being communist rebels – like Kurt Eisner, the Jewish leader of the communist rising in Munich in 1918. But they were also criticised for being selfish capitalists, since many Jews were wealthy business people. Among many, Hitler was one who blamed Germany's problems on the Jews.

Hitler's views

> If ever in power, the end of the Jews will be my first job. I shall have gallows built in Munich. Then Jews will be hanged, and will stay hanging till they stink…Then the same in other cities till Germany is cleansed of the last Jew.

Source A: *Hitler speaking to an acquaintance, Josef Hell, in 1922.*

By 1925, Hitler set out his racial views more clearly in *Mein Kampf*. He claimed that there was a hierarchy of races.

- The Aryan race was the superior race – the Herrenvolk or master race. They were portrayed as tall, blond, blue-eyed and athletic.
- Other races, such as the Slavs of Eastern Europe, were lesser races.
- Then there were the Untermenschen, or sub-humans; this included Africans.
- Worst of the Untermenschen , according to Hitler, were Gypsies and Jews. Later, Hitler deemed these Lebensunwertes – unworthy of life.

Persecution starts

When the Nazis first came to power, their persecution of Jews was limited.

- From April 1933, there were Nazi boycotts of Jewish businesses.
- From April 1933, Jews were banned from government jobs.
- From September 1933, Jews were banned from inheriting land.
- From May 1935, Jews were banned from the army.
- From June 1935, Jews were banned from restaurants.

Source B: *during the Nazi boycott of Jewish businesses, the SA put posters on the windows of Jewish shops telling people not to go in. Then they would stand outside and intimidate shoppers.*

The Nuremberg Laws

As the Nazis established themselves in power, however, persecution became worse. On 15 September 1935 the **Nuremberg Laws** were passed. These were in two parts.

- The Reich Law on Citizenship stated that only those of German blood could be German citizens. Jews lost the right to vote, hold government office or have German passports.
- The Reich Law for the Protection of German Blood and Honour forbade Jews from marrying German citizens.

From 1938, matters became more ominous.

- From April 1938, Jews had to register all possessions – making it easier for the government to confiscate them.
- From July 1938, Jews had to carry an identity card stamped with a large J for Jew.
- From July 1938, Jewish doctors, dentists and lawyers were forbidden to work for white Aryan Germans.

Kristallnacht

On 7 November 1938, a young Polish Jew, Hershel Grynszpan, went into the German embassy in Paris, randomly picked out a German, Ernst von Rath, and shot him. Grynszpan had a grievance against the Germans for the way they had treated his parents. A wave of anger swept the country and there was some violence against Jews.

Then, on 9 November, von Rath died. Goebbels told Hitler personally. He left this meeting saying that the Führer had ordered that, if Germans decided to take revenge on the Jews, the government should do nothing to prevent it. This was reported in *Der Stürmer*, the Nazi paper. Some Nazi leaders took this at face value and stood back from incidents; others took it as an order to attack the Jews. Certainly, some local SA leaders unleashed their own forces. And Heydrich, Himmler's assistant director of the SS, sent instructions to local SS groups to 'organise demonstrations' and arrest as many Jews 'as we can fit into prisons'.

So, on 9 and 10 November, gangs smashed up Jewish property and attacked Jews. Some Germans were horrified; others watched with pleasure. The official figures underestimate the violence. However, even these listed 814 shops, 171 homes and 191 synagogues destroyed. About 100 Jews were killed. The damage was so bad that these events were called **Kristallnacht** (Crystal Night) or the Night of Broken Glass.

Source C: *July 1933. This Jewish man has been accused of having a German girlfriend. They have both been forced by SA and SS members to walk the streets with signs admitting their 'crime'.*

Mob law ruled in Berlin during the afternoon and evening as hordes of hooligans went on an orgy of destruction. I have never seen an anti-Jewish outbreak as sickening as this. I saw fashionably dressed women clapping their hands and screaming with glee, while respectable women held up their children to see the 'fun'. No attempt was made by the police to stop the rioters.

Source D: from Daily Telegraph, *November 1938.*

The death of a loyal party member by the Jewish murderer has aroused anti-Jewish protests throughout the Reich. In many places Jewish shops have been smashed. The synagogues, where teachings hostile to the State and People are spread, have been set on fire. Well done to those Germans who have ensured revenge for the murder of an innocent German.

Source E: *from* Der Sturmer, *a Nazi newspaper, 10 November 1938.*

The aftermath

Goebbels blamed the Jews for starting the trouble on Kristallnacht; he said that Jews would be:

- fined 1 billion marks to pay for the damage
- banned from running shops or businesses
- banned from German schools or universities.

The SA and SS also started to round up Jews as punishment. By 12 November, 20,000 Jews had been sent to concentration camps.

Persecution came to a head in 1939.

- In January, the Reich Office for Jewish Emigration was set up. Reinhard Heydrich, head of the Gestapo, became its director. He was given the task of ridding Germany of its Jews altogether – by enforced emigration. However, progress was slow.
- From April 1939, Jews could be evicted from rented homes. After September 1939, Germany occupied Poland. Many Jews were deported to Poland and detained in fenced-off areas of towns called ghettos. In ghettos, living conditions were overcrowded and there was little food.

Who was to blame?

The Nazis kept some atrocities against Jews secret. They punished people who criticised them.

However, many Germans took part in the persecution; many others – and most other countries – did little to stop it. This is difficult to understand. A respectable middle-class woman, Frau Solmitz, attended a Nazi rally in 1933. In her diary she wrote: 'We were drunk with enthusiasm…We cried out 'Death to the Jews' and sang songs about the blood of the Jews which would squirt from our knives.' She later added the words, 'Who took that seriously then?' Some people seem to have convinced themselves that the suffering inflicted on Jews was not real; others were just too self-centred to care or too frightened to act.

Did you know?

Hitler firmly believed in weeding out the 'genetically defective' in order to purify the 'Master Race'. His ideas were based on the theories of the eugenics movement and the idea of selective breeding to improve the quality of the human population by stopping the 'unfit' from breeding.

People with one or two Jewish grandparents were called 'Mischlinge' – half-breeds. They were not to be persecuted. This was convenient for Hitler. Research into his family suggests that his own paternal grandfather may have been a Jew.

Source F: *Jews arriving at the Sachsenhausen concentration camp on 19 December 1938.*

Persecution of other minorities

Nazis believed that several other racial minorities, like the Slavs and Gypsies, were sub-human and had no place in the German community. There were about 30,000 Gypsies in Germany in the 1930s. They suffered similar persecution to the Jews.

- After 1933, Gypsies were often arrested and sent to concentration camps.
- From 1935, the Nuremberg Laws were used against Gypsies. Marriage between Gypsies and Germans was forbidden.
- In April 1939, orders were given to collect all Gypsies within enclosed and guarded ghettos inside Germany, ready to be deported.

Nazis also persecuted any people whom they believed undermined moral standards, such as homosexuals, prostitutes, Jehovah's Witnesses, alcoholics, pacifists, beggars, hooligans and persistent criminals.

- In 1935, the laws against homosexuality were strengthened. Many were sent to concentration camps; 60% of those sent to the camps died there.
- These laws also encouraged voluntary castration of homosexuals.

Nazis also persecuted those whom they believed weakened the pure German bloodline, such as the unhealthy, the disabled or the mentally ill.

- Nazis said that babies who were born disabled should be allowed to die.
- From 1933, a law was passed saying that doctors could force people to be sterilised. This law was used against people with learning difficulties, the physically or mentally disabled and alcoholics. From 1934 to 1945 about 700,000 Germans were sterilised.
- Some Germans believed that there was an unofficial policy of killing disabled children after 1933. A secret official policy was started in 1939. By 1945, 6000 disabled Germans had been killed by starvation or lethal injection.

Hildegard was obviously an afflicted child. They did not send her to school or use public services. The fear of having their child killed by the Nazis for her defect far outweighed the risk they took by not ever visiting the doctor.

Source I: *from* On Hitler's Mountain *(2005), by Irmgard Hunt, who lived in Nazi Germany. Here she is writing about a family she knew in the 1930s.*

Examination question

Explain how the lives of Jews in Germany changed in the years 1933–39.   **(8 marks)**
Tip: This is a question about *change*. There is advice about *change* questions on page 35.

In 1934, 766 males were convicted and imprisoned (for homosexuality). In 1936 it was over 4000. In 1938 it was 8000. From 1937 onwards, many of those involved were sent to concentration camps after they had served their 'regular' prison sentence.

Source G: *from a modern history book, published in 1991.*

Source H: *An NSDAP poster from about 1938. It says '60,000 Reichmarks. This is what the person suffering from hereditary defects costs the Community of Germans during his lifetime. Fellow Citizen, that is your money too.'*

Did you know?

The persecution of minorities got worse during the Second World War, which started in 1939.

It is estimated that 200,000 Gypsies and six million Jews were murdered in concentration camps by the end of the Second World War.

Know Zone
Unit 2A - Key Topic 4

In the Unit 2 exam, you will be required to answer questions on one country. You will have to answer six questions: Question 1 (a), (b), (c) and (d); either Question 2 (a) or Question 2 (b); and either Question 3 (a) or Question 3 (b).

You only have an hour and 15 minutes to answer these questions. The number of marks available for each question helps you judge how long to spend on each answer, but as a guide you might consider allocating your time as follows:

Question 1 (a)   6 minutes   Question 1 (b) 8 minutes   Question 1 (c) 12 minutes
Question 1 (d)   12 minutes   Question 2   12 minutes   Question 3   25 minutes

In addition to the 16 marks available for this question, there are 4 additional marks available for spelling, punctuation and grammar. Make sure you leave some time at the end to check these aspects of your answer. Here we are going to look Question 3.

ResultsPlus
Build Better Answers

Question 3

Tip: Both Question 3 (a) and 3 (b) will ask you to use your knowledge to make judgments on causes, effects or importance of factors. In the examination you choose to answer whichever of (a) or (b) you like the most. Do not do both (a) and (b) as you will only get marks for only one of them. Remember that this is the highest-scoring question on the paper and requires a substantial and detailed response. You will be spending around 25 minutes on this answer, so you cannot write at enormous length. However, what you should do is:

- use the examples given in the question
- think of your own causes, effects and important features
- provide factual information to support what you say about the causes, effects and important features
- make judgments on the relative importance of the causes, effects or important features.

We are going to pick a causation question and work our way through the levels until we have a high Level 4 response. The question we will use is:

Was skilful use of propaganda the main reason why Hitler had established himself in power by January 1933? Explain your answer. (16 marks)

> You may use the following information to help you with your answer.
> - Skilful use of propaganda
> - Dislike of the Weimar government
> - The economic crisis
> - Nazi policies

Student answer

I think that important reasons were Nazi policies and the skilful use of propaganda. The Nazis had policies which were popular and their use of propaganda made sure that people knew about them.

Examiner comments

I am afraid that in a 16 mark question requiring extended writing, this isn't going to score many marks! All it does is make general statements about two of the examples given in the question. That would result in a mark at the lower end of Level 1. It needs some detail to get it out of Level 1.

ResultsPlus
Build Better Answers

So let's provide that detail. The new parts are in bold.

I think that important reasons were Nazi policies and the skilful use of propaganda. The Nazis had policies which were popular and their use of propaganda made sure that people knew about them. **The Nazi policies involved giving people jobs, tearing up the Treaty of Versailles and stopping the spread of communism. They got their message across to people by holding rallies, marches, making speeches and using posters, books and newspapers.**

So now we are beginning to get some information into our answer and to write some history instead of the generalised comments we made in the previous answer. The answer develops two points so it would score towards the top of Level 2. However, although it provides factual support for the two reasons given, it doesn't bring in any new reasons or suggest how important the reasons were. For example, was one reason more important than the others?

So let's improve it. We will put the new parts in bold.

I think that important reasons were Nazi policies and the skilful use of propaganda. The Nazis had policies which were popular and their use of propaganda made sure that people knew about them. The Nazi policies involved giving people jobs, tearing up the Treaty of Versailles and stopping the spread of communism. **These policies made people want to vote for them. The policies were particularly important amongst the middle and upper classes who were frightened that the problems Germany was facing could lead to the Communists taking control. Fear of communism was definitely another reason for the Nazis winning support. But I think propaganda was more important than the policies.** They got their message across to people by holding rallies, marches, making speeches and using posters, books and newspapers. **There was no point having good policies if no one knew about them. Propaganda also fooled some people into believing the policies were better than they really were.**

We are getting to a high standard now. The answer has brought in a reason not given in the question (fear of communism), has looked at a variety of factors and decided that one of them was more important than the others (propaganda). We are now at the top of Level 3. We just need to see that the reasons are all interlinked to get to Level 4.

So let's introduce that linking by adding the following paragraph at the end of the above answer.

Student answer

However, it is true that really each reason feeds on another. The Nazi policies were popular. Why? Because there was an economic crisis as a result of the Wall St Crash. The Weimar government was already unpopular and became even more unpopular when it couldn't deal with the crisis. Communism became more popular because it offered a radical alternative to Weimar and a solution to the economic problems. The Nazis became popular because they also offered a solution which was anti-communist and which was publicised with very effective propaganda. So they are all linked, really.

Examiner comments

Lovely!

Note: remember that Question 3 is one on which your skills of written communication will be judged and the accuracy of your spelling, punctuation and grammar will be marked. Do your best to write effectively, organise coherently, and spell, punctuate and use grammar with considerable accuracy.

Welcome to exam

Revising for your exams can be a daunting prospect. Use this section of the book to get ideas, tips and practice to help you prepare as best as you can.

Zone In!

Have you ever become so absorbed in a task that it suddenly feels entirely natural? This is a feeling familiar to many athletes and performers: it's a feeling of being 'in the zone' that helps you focus and achieve your best.

Here are our top tips for getting in the zone with your revision.

- **Understand the exam process** and what revision you need to do. This will give you confidence but also help you to put things into proportion. Use the Planning Zone to create a revision plan.

- **Build your confidence** by using your revision time, not just to revise the information you need to know, but also to practise the skills you need for the examination. Try answering questions in timed conditions so that you're more prepared for writing answers in the exam.

- **Deal with distractions** by making a list of everything that might interfere with your revision and how you can deal with each issue. For example, revise in a room without a television, but plan breaks in your revision so that you can watch your favourite programmes.

- **Share your plan with friends and family** so that they know not to distract you when you want to revise. This will mean you can have more quality time with them when you aren't revising.

- **Keep healthy** by making sure you eat well and exercise, and by getting enough sleep. If your body is not in the right state, your mind won't be either – and staying up late to cram the night before the exam is likely to leave you too tired to do your best.

Planning Zone

The key to success in exams and revision often lies in the right planning, so that you don't leave anything until the last minute. Use these ideas to create your personal revision plan.

First, fill in the dates of your examinations. Check with your teacher when these are if you're not sure. Add in any regular commitments you have. This will help you get a realistic idea of how much time you have to revise.

⬇

Know your strengths and weaknesses and assign more time to topics you find difficult – don't be tempted to leave them until the last minute.

⬇

Create a revision 'checklist' using the Know Zone lists and use them to check your knowledge and skills.

⬇

Now fill in the timetable with sensible revision slots. Chunk your revision into smaller sections to make it more manageable and less daunting. Make sure you give yourself regular breaks and plan in different activities to provide some variety.

⬇

Keep to the timetable! Put your plan up somewhere visible so you can refer back to it and check that you are on track.

Know Zone

In this zone, you'll find some useful suggestions about how to structure your revision, and checklists to help you test your learning for each of the main topics. You might want to skim-read this before you start your revision planning, as it will help you think about how best to revise the content.

Remember that different people learn in different ways – some remember visually and therefore might want to think about using diagrams and other drawings for their revision, whereas others remember better through sound or through writing things out. Try to think about what works best for you by trying out some of the techniques below.

- **Summaries**: writing a summary of the information in a chapter can be a useful way of making sure you've understood it. But don't just copy it all out. Try to reduce each paragraph to a couple of sentences. Then try to reduce the couple of sentences to a few words!

- **Concept maps**: if you're a visual learner, you may find it easier to take in information by representing it visually. Draw concept maps or other diagrams. They are particularly good to show links, for example you could create a concept map which shows the effects of the Versailles Treaty on Germany. It would involve arrows pointing to such things as 'land losses', 'military losses' etc.

- **Mnemonics**: this is when you take the first letter of a series of words you want to remember and then make a new sentence.

- **Index cards**: write important events and people on index cards then test yourself on why they were important.

- **Timelines**: create a large, visual timeline and annotate it in colour.

- **Quizzes**: let's face it, learning stuff can be dull. Why not make a quiz out of it? Set a friend 20 questions to answer. Make up multiple-choice questions. You might even make up your own exam questions and see if you friend can answer them!

And then when you are ready:

- practice questions – go back through the sample exam questions in this book to see if you can answer them (without cheating!)

- try writing out some of your answers in timed conditions so that you're used to the amount of time you'll have to answer each type of question in the exam.

If you are sitting your exams from 2014 onwards, you will be sitting all your exams together at the end of your course. Make sure you know in which order you are sitting the exams, and prepare for each accordingly – check with your teacher if you're not sure. They are likely to be about a week apart, so make sure you allow plenty of revision time for each before your first exam.

Exam Zone

Know Zone Unit 2A Key Topic 1

You should know about the following things. If you can't remember any of them, just look at the page number and re-read that chapter.

76

You should know about...

❑ The Treaty of Versailles – its terms and effects **(page 7)**
❑ Reasons for German resentment of the treaty **(page 7)**
❑ How a new constitution was agreed **(page 10)**
❑ The terms and weakness of the new Weimar constitution **(page 10)**
❑ The bankruptcy of the new Weimar government **(page 12)**
❑ The occupation of the Ruhr **(page 12)**
❑ Inflation and hyperinflation **(page 12)**
❑ The main political groups in the Weimar Republic **(page 14)**
❑ The political unrest in the Weimar Republic during 1918–23 **(page 14)**
❑ Stresemann's reforms to end the currency crisis **(page 18)**
❑ Reducing reparations: the Dawes Plan and Young Plan **(page 18)**
❑ Successes abroad: the League, Locarno, Kellogg–Briand **(page 19)**
❑ The causes and effects of the Great Depression in Germany **(page 22)**

Key people

Do you know why these people are important?

Heinrich Brüning

Georges Clemenceau

Friedrich Ebert

Matthias Erzberger

David Lloyd George

Paul von Hindenburg

Gustav Stresemann

Woodrow Wilson

Test your spelling

Remember that in questions 2 and 3, the accuracy of your spelling is one element of your answer that will be assessed. Make sure you can spell the key events, ideas and people listed above, and the following terms from this key topic:

abdicate

autocracy

bankruptcy

capitalism

coalition

colony

communism

constitution

demilitarised

democrat/democratic

diktat

Dolchstoss

economic

fascism

Freikorps

(hyper)inflation

military

parliament

plebiscite

political

proportional representation

Reichsrat

Reichstag

reparations

republic

socialism

territory

Weimar

Key events

November 1918 Kaiser abdicated **(page 6)**

11 November 1918 Armistice signed **(page 7)**

January 1919 Spartacist uprisings **(pages 16–17)**

28 June 1919 Germans signed Treaty of Versailles **(page 7)**

August 1919 New constitution drawn up **(page 10)**

1920 Kapp Putsch **(page 17)**

1923 Munich Putsch **(page 17)**

1923 French occupation of the Ruhr **(page 12)**

September 1923 Gustav Stresemann appointed Chancellor **(page 18)**

November 1923 Rentenmark issued **(page 18)**

April 1924 Dawes Plan agreed **(page 18)**

1925 Paul von Hindenburg became president **(page 21)**

October 1925 Locarno Pact signed **(page 19)**

September 1926 Germany accepted as member of the League of Nations **(page 20)**

August 1928 Kellogg–Briand Pact signed **(page 20)**

August 1929 Young Plan agreed **(page 19)**

3 October 1929 Stresemann died **(page 21)**

24 October 1929 Wall Street Crash **(page 22)**

You should know about the following things. If you can't remember any of them, just look at the page number and re-read that chapter.

You should know about...

❏ Hitler's youth in Austria **(page 26)**

❏ Hitler's move to Germany and service in the First World War **(page 27)**

❏ Hitler's first political activity **(page 27)**

❏ The German Workers' Party (DAP) when Hitler joined **(page 28)**

❏ The early Nazi Party, its aims and early features, including the SA **(page 28)**

❏ The causes, events and results of the Munich Putsch **(page 30)**

❏ The political ideas of the Nazi Party after 1924 **(page 32)**

❏ How Hitler improved the organisation and finance of the NSDAP **(page 34)**

❏ The growth of the SA; the start of the SS **(page 34)**

❏ Joseph Goebbels and Nazi propaganda **(page 34)**

❏ Weak Nazi results in national elections 1924–29 **(page 35)**

❏ How much and why support for the Nazis grew, 1929–32 **(page 36)**

❏ Who supported the Nazis, 1929–32 **(page 36)**

❏ Hitler standing for election as president **(page 40)**

❏ A series of chancellors falling from power **(page 40)**

❏ Hitler becoming chancellor in January 1933 **(page 41)**

Key people

Do you know why these people are important?

Heinrich Brüning	Rudolf Hess	Kurt von Schleicher
Anton Drexler	Adolf Hitler	Julius Streicher
Joseph Goebbels	Franz von Papen	
Hermann Goering	Ernst Röhm	

Test your spelling

Remember that in questions 2 and 3, the accuracy of your spelling is one element of your answer that will be assessed. Make sure you can spell the key events, ideas and people listed above, and the following terms from this key topic:

coalition	Lebensraum	Reichstag
(hyper)inflation	nationalism	totalitarianism
Kaiser	propaganda	treason

Key events

20 April 1889 Hitler born **(page 26)**

15 January 1919 German Workers' Party (DAP) founded **(page 27)**

7 August 1920 DAP became National Socialist German Workers' Party (NSDAP) **(page 29)**

1921 Hitler became NSDAP's Führer **(page 29)**

1921 Sturmabteilung (SA) created **(page 29)**

November 1923 Munich Putsch **(page 30)**

27 February 1925 Nazi Party re-launched **(page 34)**

1925 *Mein Kampf* first published **(page 31)**

1925 Schutzstaffel (SS) set up **(page 34)**

October 1929 Wall Street Crash **(page 40)**

March 1932 Hitler stood for election as president **(page 40)**

April 1932 Brüning removed as chancellor **(page 40)**

May 1932 von Papen made chancellor of new coalition that included NSDAP **(page 40)**

November 1932 von Papen resigned, following election; replaced by Schleicher **(page 41)**

30 January 1933 Hitler appointed chancellor **(page 41)**

Know Zone Unit 2A Key Topic 3

You should know about the following things. If you can't remember any of them, just look at the page number and re-read that chapter.

You should know about...

❑ The Reichstag fire and the election of March 1933 **(page 45)**

❑ The Enabling Act, the banning of political parties and trade unions **(page 46)**

❑ The Night of the Long Knives **(page 48)**

❑ The death of President Hindenburg **(page 49)**

❑ Himmler, the SS and the Gestapo **(page 50)**

❑ Nazi concentration camps and the law courts **(page 51)**

❑ Repression of the Church in Nazi Germany **(page 52)**

❑ How the Nazis used censorship to ban information and ideas which they didn't like **(page 54)**

❑ How the Nazis used propaganda to publicise information and ideas which they wanted to promote **(page 54)**

Key people

Do you know why these people are important?

Marinus van der Lubbe

Hermann Goering

Ernst Röhm

Heinrich Himmler

Ludwig Müller

Martin Niemöller

Test your spelling

Remember that in questions 2 and 3, the accuracy of your spelling is one element of your answer that will be assessed. Make sure you can spell the key events, ideas and people listed above, and the following terms from this key topic:

censorship	journalist
chancellor	nationalist
communist	parliament
constitution	plebiscite
democratic	propaganda
dictator	racial
Führer	totalitarian
Gestapo	

Key events

27 February 1933 Reichstag building destroyed by fire **(page 45)**

5 March 1933 Hitler gets two-thirds majority in election **(page 45)**

March 1933 First Nazi concentration camp opened at Dachau **(page 51)**

May 1933 trade unions banned and strikes made illegal **(page 46)**

July 1933 all political parties except NSDAP made illegal **(page 47)**

July 1933 Concordat agreed with Pope **(page 52)**

January 1934 Länder parliaments abolished **(page 47)**

30 June 1934 The Night of the Long Knives **(page 48)**

2 August 1934 Death of President Hindenburg; Hitler declared Führer **(page 49)**

1936 Olympic Games held in Berlin **(page 57)**

1937 Pastors' Emergency League banned **(page 53)**

Know Zone Unit 2A Key Topic 4

You should know about the following things. If you can't remember any of them, just look at the page number and re-read that chapter.

79

Exam Zone

You should know about...

- ❑ Schools and youth movements in Nazi Germany **(page 61)**
- ❑ Youth opposition to Hitler **(page 61)**
- ❑ Nazi views on the role of women **(page 62)**
- ❑ Nazi policies to increase marriage and childbirth **(page 63)**
- ❑ Opposition to Nazi views on women **(page 62)**
- ❑ Hitler's policies for German workers **(page 64)**
- ❑ Hitler's policies for Germany's unemployed **(page 64)**
- ❑ Hitler's policy of rearmament and its economic effects **(page 65)**
- ❑ Rises in employment, wage levels and consumer spending **(page 66)**
- ❑ Changes in working conditions **(page 66)**
- ❑ Rises in prices **(page 66)**
- ❑ The overall effect of the above three changes on German living standards **(page 66)**
- ❑ The persecution of the Jews and other minorities in Nazi Germany **(page 68)**
- ❑ Nazi persecution of other minority groups **(page 68)**

Key people

Do you know why these people are important?

Kurt Eisner   Reinhard Heydrich

Hershel Grynszpan

Test your spelling

Remember that in questions 2 and 3, the accuracy of your spelling will be assessed. Make sure you can spell the events, ideas and people listed above, and the following terms from this key topic:

anti-Semitism   gypsy

Aryan   persecution

ghetto   rearmament

                           synagogue

Key events

1933 Law for the Encouragement of Marriage introduced **(page 63)**

1933 DAF (German Labour Front) set up after trade unions abolished **(page 64)**

1933 RAD (National Labour Service) set up **(page 64)**

1933 Law passed allowing doctors to force sterilisation **(page 71)**

April 1933 Nazi boycotts of Jewish businesses began **(page 68)**

April 1933 Jews banned from government jobs **(page 68)**

September 1933 Jews banned from inheriting land **(page 68)**

1935 Lebensborn programme introduced **(page 63)**

1935 Six months' service in RAD became compulsory **(page 64)**

1935 Laws against homosexuality strengthened **(page 71)**

May 1935 Jews banned from army **(page 68)**

June 1935 Jews banned from restaurants **(page 68)**

15 September 1935 Nuremberg Laws passed **(page 69)**

1936 Hitler issued a secret memo regarding the Four Year Plan **(page 65)**

April 1938 Jews had to register all possessions **(page 69)**

July 1938 Jews had to carry identity cards; Jewish doctors, dentists and lawyers forbidden to work for white Aryan Germans **(page 69)**

November 1938 Kristallnacht **(page 69)**

January 1939 Reich Office for Jewish Emigration set up **(page 70)**

April 1939 orders given to collect Gypsies for deportation **(page 71)**

Don't Panic Zone

As the day of the exam gets closer, many students tend to go into panic mode, either working long hours without really giving their brain a chance to absorb information, or giving up and staring blankly at the wall.

Look over your revision notes and go through the checklists to remind yourself of the main areas you need to know about. Don't try to cram in too much new information at the last minute and don't stay up late revising – you'll do better if you get a good night's sleep.

Exam Zone

What to expect in the exam paper

You will have 1 hour and 15 minutes in the examination.

Question 1 is divided into four sub-questions and you should answer all four.

1(a) is worth 4 marks.

You are given a source and asked what you can learn from it. You need to work out something that is not actually stated in the source. If the source says *'Hitler used the Gestapo to intimidate his enemies'* and you are asked what you can learn about life under Hitler you could say *'it was tough because he took harsh measures against his opponents like using the Gestapo'.*
We call that a 'supported inference'. You can see an example of this type of question explained on page 29.

1(b) is worth 6 marks.

You will be asked to describe something that happened. Sometimes the question says 'key features', which means you need to group your facts.

So if you are asked for the key features of Stresemann's work, you ought to think:

'improved the economy', 'brought back confidence', 'improved relations with other countries'.

Then you give some facts about each of these.

You can see an example of this type of question explained on page 21.

1(c) is worth 8 marks.

It asks you to explain the effects or consequences of an action or event.

So if you are asked for the consequences of the Great Depression, you don't write about the Great Depression itself, you write about what it made happen.

You can see an example of this type of question explained on page 23.

1(d) is worth 8 marks.

It asks you to explain why something happened.

So if you are asked why the Weimar Republic collapsed in 1929, make sure you don't write about 'how' it collapsed.

Question 2 is worth 8 marks and is divided into two parts. You should answer either part (a) or part (b).
It asks you to explain how something changed or came to happen. So if you are asked how the Nazi Party developed from 1920 to 1928, you start in 1920 and give the details of the changes.

You can see an example of this type of question explained on page 35.

Your answer for this question will also be marked for spelling, punctuation and grammar: there are up to 3 additional marks available for this aspect of your writing.

Question 3 is worth 16 marks and is divided into two parts. You should answer either part (a) or part (b).
It asks you to explain whether one reason was more important than other reasons for making something happen. The good news is that it gives you four reasons.

So if you are asked whether the police state was the most important reason for Hitler staying in power in the period 1933–39, you write about how the police state helped him stay in power. Then you write about how the other reasons you are given help him (and any reasons you can think of for yourself). Then you do the clever bit and see if you can make a case for any reason or reasons being more important than others.

You can see an example of this type of question explained on page 39.

Your answer for this question will also be marked for spelling, punctuation and grammar: there are up to 4 additional marks available for this aspect of your writing.

Meet the exam paper

In this exam you will write all of your answers in the spaces provided on the exam paper. It's important that you use a black pen and that you indicate clearly which questions you have answered where a choice is provided – instructions will be given on the paper. Try to make your handwriting as legible as possible.

This diagram shows the front cover and two pages from a sample exam paper. These instructions, information and advice will always appear on the front of the paper. It is worth reading it carefully now as well as in the exam. Check you understand it and ask your teacher about anything you are not sure of.

Print your surname here, and your other names afterwards. This is an additional safeguard to ensure that the exam board awards the marks to the right candidate.

Here you fill in the school's exam number.

The Unit 2 exam lasts 1 hour 15 minutes. Plan your time accordingly.

Make sure that you understand exactly which questions from which sections you should attempt.

Here you fill in your personal exam number. Take care to write it accurately.

In this box, the examiner will write the total marks you have achieved in the exam paper.

Don't feel that you have to fill the answer space provided. Everybody's handwriting varies, so a long answer from you may take up as much space a short answer from someone else.

Remember that in Questions 2 and 3 your spelling, punctuation and grammar will be assessed, and that in Question 3 the quality of your written communication will be assessed. Take time to check your spelling, punctuation and grammar and to make sure that you have expressed yourself clearly.

Write your name here

Surname

Other names

Centre Number

Candidate Number

Edexcel GCSE

History A (The Making of the Modern World)
Unit 2: Modern World Depth Study
Option 2A: Germany, 1918–39

Sample Assessment Material
Time: 1 hour 15 minutes

Paper Reference
5HA02/2A

You do not need any other materials.

Total Marks

Instructions

● Use **black** ink or ball-point pen.
● **Fill in the boxes** at the top of this page with your name, centre number and candidate number.
● Answer **six** questions (1(a), (b), (c), (d), 2(a) or 2(b), 3(a) or 3(b)).
● Answer the questions in the spaces provided
  – there may be more space than you need.

Information

● The total mark for this paper is 57.
● The marks for **each** question are shown in brackets
  – use this as a guide as to how much time to spend on each question.
● Questions labelled with an **asterisk** (*) are ones where the quality of your written communication will be assessed.
● The marks available for spelling, punctuation and grammar are clearly indicated.

Advice

● Read each question carefully before you start to answer it.
● Keep an eye on the time.
● Check your answers if you have time at the end.

W41862A
©2012 Pearson Education Ltd.
1/1

Turn over ▶

PEARSON

Germany, 1918–39

Answer Questions 1(a) to (d), then Question 2(a) OR 2(b) and then Question 3(a) OR 3(b).

Question 1 – you must answer all parts of this question.

Study Source A.

Source A: From a history of Germany, published in 1996.

> The Spartacists tried to seize power on 5 January 1919 but they were doomed to failure. The day before they began their rising, Ebert created a volunteer force of 4,000 soldiers. Known as the Free Corps, they were hard men who hated communists and liked a fight. They were well disciplined, fully equipped and ruthless. They retook all the Spartacist occupied buildings in Berlin and captured and shot the two Spartacist leaders.

(a) What can you learn from Source A about the reasons for the failure of the Spartacist uprising of January 1919?

(4)

You need to answer questions 1, 2 and 3. You should answer all parts of question 1, but for question 2 and question 3, you should answer either (a) or (b).

Question 1 will provide you with a source to study before answering part (a). Read the information about it carefully. When you answer you should always say what the source tells you and give a reason for it.

The number of marks available for each question is given on the right.

A good answer for 1 (b) will make more than one point (the question says problems) and support or explain each point with some detail.

(b) Describe the economic problems Germany experienced in the years 1919–22.

(6)

2

(c) Explain the effects of hyperinflation in 1923 on Germany and its people.

(8)

The question says 'effects' so make sure you describe at least two effects, and three if you can.

(d) Explain why there was a period of recovery for Germany in the years 1924-29.

(8)

1 (d) is a cause question, so make sure your answer has more than one cause and, for each cause you include, explain why it was a cause or how it worked.

Answer EITHER Question 2(a) OR 2(b).

Spelling, punctuation and grammar will be assessed in this question.

EITHER

2 (a) Explain how the Nazi Party developed in the years 1920–28.

(8)

OR

2 (b) Explain how the position of women in Germany changed in the years 1933–39.

(8)

Indicate which question you are answering by marking a cross in the box ☒. If you change your mind, put a line through the box ☒ and then indicate your new question with a cross ☒.

Chosen Question Number: **Question 2(a)** ☐   **Question 2(b)** ☒

The live question paper will contain one further page of lines.

(Total for spelling, punctuation and grammar = 3 marks)

(Total for Question 2 = 11 marks)

6

W 4 1 8 6 2 A 0 6 0 8

Remember to check your spelling, punctuation and grammer when you see this highlighted.

Your explanation should always include more than one reason or feature. Make sure you support or explain each feature and if you can, explain how the features link together.

Remember, in question 2 you have a choice. Look at both parts and decide which one to answer, then make sure you put an x in the right box to show which question you have answered.

In question 3 you also have to choose to answer either part (a) or part (b).

Remember to check your spelling, punctuation and grammar when you see this highlighted

Answer EITHER Question 3(a) OR 3(b).

Spelling, punctuation and grammar will be assessed in this question.

EITHER

*3 (a) Was the use of propaganda the main reason Hitler was able to establish a dictatorship of the Nazi Party in the years 1935–39? Explain your answer.

(16)

You may use the following in your answer and any other information of your own.

- The use of propaganda
- The use of censorship
- The police state
- Persecution of the churches

OR

*3 (b) Were attacks on Jewish businesses the worst effects of Nazi persecution of the Jews in the years 1933–39? Explain your answer.

(16)

You may use the following in your answer and any other information of your own.

- Attacks on Jewish businesses
- Education
- 1935 Nuremberg Laws
- 1938 Kristallnacht

Use your time wisely. This question is worth 16 marks, one third of all the marks for this exam.

(Total for spelling, punctuation and grammar = 4 marks)
(Total for Question 3 = 20 marks)

Indicate which question you are answering by marking a cross in the box ⊠. If you change your mind, put a line through the box ⊠ and then indicate your new question with a cross ⊠.

Chosen Question Number: **Question 3(a)** ☐   **Question 3(b)** ☐

Make sure you put an x in the correct box to show which question you have answered.

The live question paper will contain a further three pages of lines.

TOTAL FOR PAPER = 57 MARKS

This question asks you to make a judgment. You get some help in the information provided with the question. You must show the examiner that you understand all the things on the list and add some of your own if you can. You must also make sure you write about which was the main reason or the worst effects. To do this you have to compare the importance of the things you are writing about.

2 A 0 7 0 8

7

Zone Out

This section provides answers to the most common questions students have about what happens after they complete their exams. For more information, visit www.examzone.co.uk.

When will my results be published?

Results for GCSE summer examinations are issued on the third Thursday in August. January exam results are issued in March and March exam results issued in April.

If you are sitting your exams from 2014 onwards, there will no longer be January sittings: you will sit all of your exams in June.

Can I get my results online?

Visit www.resultsplusdirect.co.uk, where you will find detailed student results information including the 'Edexcel Gradeometer' which demonstrates how close you were to the nearest grade boundary.

I haven't done as well as I expected. What can I do now?

First of all, talk to your teacher. After all the teaching that you have had, and the tests and internal examinations you have done, he/she is the person who best knows what grade you are capable of achieving. Take your results slip to your subject teacher, and go through the information on it in detail. If you both think that there is something wrong with the result, the school or college can apply to see your completed examination paper and then, if necessary, ask for a re-mark immediately.

Bear in mind that the original mark can be confirmed or lowered, as well as raised, as a result of a re-mark.

Can I resit this unit?

If you are sitting your exams before 2014, you may resit a unit once prior to claiming certification for the qualification. If you are sitting your exams from 2014 onwards, you will not be able to resit any of the exams.

How many times can I resit a unit?

You may resit a unit once prior to claiming certification for the qualification. The best available result for each contributing unit will count towards the final grade. If you wish to resit after you have completed all the assessment requirements of the course, you will have to retake at least 40% of the assessment requirements (that means two units). Please note that if you take a resit as one of the two units in your final assessment, the score you get will be counted – even if your original score was higher.

Glossary

Term	Definition
autarky	Hitler's desire for Germany to be self-sufficient and not dependent on imports.
birth rate	The number of children born per 1000 people in the country.
blueprint	A clear plan.
central government	That part of a political system which governs the whole country from the state capital.
chancellor	The leader of the government in the Weimar Republic.
checks and balances	Limiting the powers of each part of a political system so that no one part is too powerful.
coalition	Several groups, like political parties, agreeing to work together.
conspiracy	A plot or secret plan by a group of people to do something illegal.
constitution	The rules which say how a country should be governed.
decree	In the Weimar Republic, this was an official order, with the force of law, issued by the government, without consulting the Reichstag.
democratic	Controlled by the people.
depression	A downturn in trade. Less is bought and sold; this causes falls in profits, more bankrupt businesses and more unemployment.
diktat	An agreement forced on someone.
figurehead	The leading figure, who sets the image for a country or an organisation.
Freikorps	Ex-soldiers used by the government of the Weimar Republic as a military force to put down unrest, especially from left-wing political groups.
general elections	Popular votes to elect members of parliament – in the Weimar Republic, to elect members of the Reichstag.
Gestapo	The Geheime Staatspolizei, the Nazi Party's non-uniformed secret police.
inflation	Rising prices – it means that money buys less and is therefore worth less.
Kristallnacht	Literally, 'crystal night' – or night of broken glass; a time of violence against Jews and Jewish properties.
League of Nations	An international body, made up of most countries of the world in the 1920s and 1930s, which tried to solve disputes by peace rather than war.
living standards	The quality of people's lives, measured by their wealth, health or happiness.
local government	The government of individual towns, counties or parts of a state by the people who live there.

Term	Definition
November Criminals	The term used to criticise the politicians who ended the war, in November 1918.
Nuremberg Laws	A set of laws, passed in 1935, which persecuted Jews and other minority groups.
one party state	A country which allows only one political party, which holds all government posts.
persecution	Planned and persistent mistreatment.
plebiscite	A special public vote arranged to make a key decision.
power vacuum	A situation where nobody has control, making it possible for someone to step in and take over.
president	The head of state in the Weimar Republic.
presidential elections	The popular vote taken in the Weimar Republic to elect the country's president.
proportional representation	An electoral system in which a party is given a number of representatives in direct proportion to the total number of votes for that party.
rallies	Big public meetings, used to increase enthusiasm or support for an organisation or movement.
rearmament	The policy of increasing armed forces and weapons in preparation for war.
Reichsrat	The less powerful house of the German parliament in the Weimar Republic.
Reichstag	The more powerful house of the German parliament in the Weimar Republic.
reparations	The compensation which the Allies made Germany pay at the end of the First World War, because they said Germany caused the war.
Schutzstaffel	The SS, a military group set up in 1925 as a personal bodyguard for Hitler.
state of emergency	A crisis so great that the normal rules of governing are suspended and the rulers are given extra powers to allow strong government.
stock exchange	A place where people buy and sell shares in businesses.
Sturmabteilung	The SA or storm troopers; they were the armed private army of the Nazi Party, used to protect Nazis and intimidate other political groups.
totalitarian state	A country where the government controls all aspects of society and people's lives.
treason	The crime of betraying one's country.

Acknowledgements

Pearson Education Limited
Edinburgh Gate
Harlow
Essex
CM20 2JE
England
© Pearson Education 2009

The right of John Child to be identified as the author of this work has been asserted by him in accordance with the Copyright, Designs and Patents Act 1988.

ISBN 978-1-84690-547-6
The publishers are grateful to Anna Jones and James Rich for their contributions to the book.

Designed by eMC Design Ltd

Illustrations by Peter Bull Studio

15 14 13 12
10 9 8 7 6

Printed in Malaysia, KHL-CTP

The publisher would like to thank the following for their kind permission to reproduce their photographs:

(Key: b-bottom; c-centre; l-left; r-right; t-top)

akg-images Ltd: 9, 12b, 12t, 14, 16, 19, 31, 46, 48; Coll. Archiv f.Kunst & Geschichte 6, 10, 36, 38; Ullstein Bild 28; Westfalisches Schulmuseum 11, 23; **Bildarchiv Preussischer Kulturbesitz:** 18, 21, 30, 45, 63; **Bridgeman Art Library Ltd:** Biblioteque Nationale, Paris, France 20; Property of the Federal Republic of Germany / Adolf Wissel 62t; Kunstgewerbe Museum, Zurich, Switzerland 15; Peter Newark Military Pictures 34, 37b, 40, 44, 52t, 56, 57bl, 57tr, 61b; **Corbis:** 62b, 68, 70; Austrian Archives 60, 61t; Bettmann 64; Hulton-Deutsch Collection 27; **Deutsches Historisches Museum, Berlin:** 71; **Getty Images:** Hulton Archive 17; Imagno 22t, 55; Keystone 69; Roger Viollet 52b; **Solo Syndication:** Associated Newspapers Ltd / David Low, The Star, 2 Feb 1921, British Cartoon Archive, University of Kent, www.cartoons.ac.uk 7, / David Low, Evening Standard, 19 Sep 1931, British Cartoon Archive, University of Kent, www.cartoons.ac.uk 22b, / David Low, Evening Standard, 3 Jul 1934, British Cartoon Archive, University of Kent, www.cartoons.ac.uk 49, / David Low, Evening Standard, 19 Oct 1934, British Cartoon Archive, University of Kent, www.cartoons.ac.uk 53, / David Low, Evening Standard, 7 Feb 1938, British Cartoon Archive, University of Kent, www.cartoons. ac.uk 65, / David Low, Evening Standard, 30 Dec 1936, British Cartoon Archive, University of Kent, www. cartoons.ac.uk 67; **Express Syndication:** Sidney 'George' Strube, Daily Express, 13 Jul 1933, British Cartoon Archive, University of Kent, www.cartoons.ac.uk 47, Sidney 'George' Strube, Daily Express, 24 Jul 1935, British Cartoon Archive, University of Kent, www.cartoons.ac.uk 54; **TopFoto:** 50; Roger Viollet 26; Topham / Punch Limited 41; Ullstein Bild 29, 32, 33, 37t, 39

Cover images: *Front:* **Getty Images:** Time & Life Pictures

Disclaimer